Tsongkhapa's
Praise for Dependent Relativity

TSONGKHAPA'S
Praise for Dependent Relativity

Lobsang Gyatso
and Graham Woodhouse

WISDOM PUBLICATIONS • BOSTON

Wisdom Publications
199 Elm Street
Somerville, MA 02214 USA
www.wisdompubs.org

Library of Congress Cataloging-in-Publication Data

Blo-bzaṅ-rgya-mtsho, Phu-khaṅ Dge-bśes.
  Tsongkhapa's Praise for dependent relativity / Losang Gyatso and Graham Woodhouse.
    p. cm.
  Includes translations from Tibetan.
  ISBN 0-86171-264-1 (pbk. : alk. paper)
  1. Tsoṅ-kha-pa Blo-bzaṅ-grags-pa, 1357–1419. Rten 'brel bstod pa. 2. Śūnyatā. I. Woodhouse, Graham, 1952– II. Tsoṅ-kha-pa Blo-bzaṅ-grags-pa, 1357–1419. Rten 'brel bstod pa. English. III. Title.
  BQ4275.B58 2011
  294.3'85—dc23
                          2011030584

ISBN 978-0-86171-264-9
eBook ISBN 978-0-86171-721-7

15 14 13 12 11
5 4 3 2 1

Cover design by TLJE. Interior design by Gopa&Ted2, Inc. Set in Sabon LT Std 10.25/14. Cover photo: Solway Beach, Cumbria, UK. Reproduced with the kind permission of the photog- rapher, Ally McGurk: www.flickr.com/allybeag.

Wisdom Publications' books are printed on acid-free paper and meet the guidelines for perma- nence and durability of the Committee on Production Guidelines for Book Longevity of the Council on Library Resources.

Printed in United States of America.

 This book was produced with environmental mindfulness. We have elected to print this title on 30% PCW recycled paper. As a result, we have saved the following resources: 8 trees, 4 million BTUs of energy, 824 lbs. of greenhouse gases, 3,716 gallons of water, and 235 lbs. of solid waste. For more information, please visit our website, www.wisdompubs.org. This paper is also FSC® certified. For more information, please visit www.fscus.org. Environmental impact estimates were made using the Environmental Paper Network Paper Calculator. For more information visit www.papercalcu- lator.org.

Contents

Publisher's Acknowledgment

T HE PUBLISHER gratefully acknowledges the generous help of the Hershey Family Foundation in sponsoring the publication of this book.

Preface

The voice expressing virtuous words,
the mind absorbed in virtuous thoughts.
Tibetan saying

TSONGKHAPA'S *Praise for Dependent Relativity* is a masterpiece whose full glory is perhaps best appreciated when it is sung in unison with others. Its eloquent beauty lends itself not just to silent reflection in tranquility but also to chanting in the act of group prayer. My wish, therefore, has been to produce an English version that is fully chantable.

As others before me have noted, solo performance scarcely exists in the public realm of Tibetan Buddhist music. Group vocalization, usually by everyone in attendance, is the more common practice. The effect is more sonorous than tuneful, since the melodies are of the minimal kind we associate with chanting rather than singing.

Music in the Tibetan Buddhist tradition is, of course, sacred music, so sensual enjoyment of it is not an end in itself. Its true purpose is to lead us beyond the world. In this context, chanting and temple music are primarily an offering to the buddhas. The buddhas abide in delight, but, it is said, greater still is their joy when people devotedly apply themselves to the Dharma and make such offerings with pure-minded resolve. Then the Buddha's blessings flow forth ever more abundantly. When we offer such a song of praise as this, we will receive more readily their direct inspiration, and we will attune more easily to their transcendent message.

Participating in Tibetan sacred chants has an extraordinary power to move the mind. We yearn to escape the limitations of our own confusion, and our hearts lift up in gladness when we celebrate Tsongkhapa's wisdom-insight using his very speech. When many voices intone his verses together, as they have done in the prayer halls of Tibet for six hundred years, there is a multiplying effect, nourishing the faith of those who have not yet fathomed the profound meaning of the words and refreshing the determination of those who are dedicated to study and meditation, gradually filling up that great reservoir of merit needed to develop universal compassion and enter the path.

Such chanting has been most inspiring for me when attending a *tsog* (prayer service) in one of the great Tibetan monastic universities now relocated in exile in tropical South India. There, even the molecules of the roof beams of the great assembly hall vibrate to a swelling chorus of hundreds of monks urging on the victory of compassion over the forces of darkness. When the monks finally sustain a soaring high note, which hangs there like an eagle in the wind, for a moment it feels almost as if entry into the nondual might not be so far off! The splendid, deep roaring of the chant leader's multiphonic *basso profundo* fades back in, commencing the next verse. The high note dies away into echoes. Once again another crescendo of sound slowly gathers amplitude.

When the monks or nuns are chanting just right, the chant master says approvingly, "One voice, one note." When someone is spoiling the harmony, the reprimand is "Yours is just sheep noise, goat noise!"

During my time at the Institute of Buddhist Dialectics in Dharamsala, India, I never felt the continual application of reasoning in debate to be an arid or sterile exercise, pointlessly intellectual. Rather, in that lively and good-humored atmosphere, a better way of thinking gradually began to shape the stubborn, unwilling mind. However, I often found strenuous and demanding the unrelenting quest for truths too subtle to be merely grasped at. At such times, the current of energy set flowing by Tsongkhapa's *Praise for Dependent Relativity* and other such noble compositions sounding forth from many throats in the prayer assembly was revitalizing, a solace for drooping spirits and an ideal antidote for brain fatigue.

About Lobsang Gyatso

Only after 1959, when Tibet was overrun and many Tibetans were driven into exile, did Westerners in any numbers begin to appreciate Tsongkhapa's version of what exactly constitutes an insight into reality, the final view that brings peace. One of the great teachers of the earlier Westerners visiting the Tibetan exile community in India was Venerable Lobsang Gyatso, the primary author of the commentary that here accompanies Tsongkhapa's verses. By that time Lobsang Gyatso was director of the Institute of Buddhist Dialectics, which His Holiness the Dalai Lama had founded in 1973 in response to his appeal.

Lobsang Gyatso was born in the Kongjo Rawa region of Kham province in the far southeast of Tibet in 1928. In his early twenties, he went for higher Buddhist studies to Lhasa and entered the great monastic university of Drepung, established at the behest of Tsongkhapa in 1416. In March 1959, Lobsang Gyatso fled Lhasa after the climactic act of the Chinese takeover of Tibet, their artillery bombardment of the capital following the Dalai Lama's secret departure. He made a harrowing escape to India in the footsteps of the Dalai Lama.

Lobsang Gyatso responded to the trauma of exile by enrolling in the first batch of monks to be trained as school teachers in response to the urgent needs of the Tibetan refugee community. He worked for eight years for the Central Tibetan Schools Administration, primarily at Mussoorie. This was the first stage of a career marked by assiduous and farsighted efforts for the educationally deprived, for Tibetan society in its long drawn-out crisis, and for all those interested in Buddhist philosophy, whatever their background. During his quarter of a century as director of the Institute of Buddhist Dialectics, his selfless devotion, acuity, poverty, fearlessness, and open-mindedness served a remarkably broad range of students from the Land of Snows and from both East and West. There he became my dear and respected teacher as well.

As Lobsang Gyatso himself wrote, it was His Holiness the Dalai Lama who really inspired him to extinguish self-centered inclinations and put all his energy into working for the benefit of others. Even his tragic death at the hands of assailants in his own room at the Institute in 1997 was in the loyal service of the Dalai Lama. Particularly since they were classmates of mine at the Institute of Buddhist Dialectics, I would like to recall the two young men who were murdered with him, Ngawang Lodroe and Losang Ngawang, young minds glowing brightly like fresh butter lamps before a venerable shrine.

The following commentary originated in a series of lectures given by Lobsang Gyatso to an audience of Westerners at Tushita Retreat Centre, Dharamsala. To these, I have made significant additions and clarifications to throw what light I can on questions I have often been asked when teaching *Praise for Dependent Relativity* myself. Thus the commentary is a joint effort, though final responsibility for its accuracy necessarily rests with me.

About the Translation of the Verses

Tsongkhapa shows in his prose works a mastery of the grandiloquent periodic sentence. His verses, on the other hand, achieve their intensity by combining the rhythm of poetry with sheer conciseness. In verse, the Tibetan language's tolerance for a minimal use of verb auxiliaries, case markers, conjunctions, and pronouns permits a very brief seven-syllable line and encourages a fine tautness of expression that is a challenge to match in English. In the original, *Praise for Dependent Relativity*'s four-line stanzas have only twenty-eight syllables each, except for one stanza in the middle and the concluding six, which have thirty-six syllables, in four lines of nine syllables each.

I have no argument with other modes of translation, recasting, modernizing, paraphrasing, adding, and subtracting, but of all the translations of Tibetan religious verse into English that I have seen, rarely indeed has the translator even attempted the terseness, pithiness, and rhythmic intensity that is the peculiar stamp of Tibetan Buddhist poetry and half the source of the uplift and delight that *Praise for Dependent Relativity* inspires. So, while being as faithful as possible to the meaning, I have tried to concentrate on just those qualities.

As far as I have seen, Tibetan translations always render Sanskrit Buddhist verse into regular meter, though no doubt Tibetan verse forms are very different from Sanskrit ones. As the wheel of Dharma rolls from place to place, and the time of English has come, it seemed to me that a free-verse translation would be unfaithful to *Praise for Dependent Relativity*, however much of the content it conveyed. Thus I have tried to imitate in whatever pale way something of the style of Tsongkhapa's Tibetan, which sings like a mountain stream, brimming with the inspiring force of poetic rhythm. It is my hope at least that English speakers too can now lift up their voices and chant the poem together, and thereby attune both heart and mind more readily to the insights and ideals it contains.

In this translation, I have added one extra syllable per line. The iambic tetrameter serves to imitate the conciseness of the Tibetan seven-syllable line, and the iambic pentameter substitutes for the nine-syllable line. One way to chant it is simply to raise the pitch of the voice slightly on the sixth syllable of each line. Gradually slowing down from verse 49 (and increasing the volume!) helps to make verse 52 an impressive climax. Verses 53–58 go quickly with no variation in pitch and with the main emphasis on the last syllable of each line.

The short form of the title in Tibetan is *Rten 'brel bstod pa*, not *Rten 'byung bstod pa*. *'Brel* means "related" and *'byung* means "arising" or "originating." I have therefore translated the title as *Praise for Dependent Relativity* in contrast to other recent translators who have preferred *Praise for Dependent Arising* or *Dependent Origination*. In *Praise for Dependent Relativity* and prose works such as the *Great Treatise on the Stages of the Path*, Tsongkhapa makes varied use of three terms, *rten 'byung*, *rten 'brel*, and *rten cing 'brel bar 'byung ba*, as the Tibetan equivalents of the one Sanskrit word *pratityasamutpada*. Though the three are synonymous, rather than translate them all simply as "dependent arising" or "arising in dependence" and so on as others have done, I have tried to reflect Tsongkhapa's preference for a variety of terms. I have used "arising in dependence" and so on only for *rten 'byung* and "dependent relativity" or "relativity" and so on for *rten 'brel* and *rten cing 'brel bar 'byung ba*. The three terms occur so frequently in *Praise for Dependent Relativity* that to translate them all in the same way would be monotonous.

Sources of Guidance and Acknowledgments

In addition to the kind, indispensable explanations of many living teachers, I have mainly followed two written commentaries in deciphering the meaning of the verses. The first, by Gen Lamrimpa Ngawang Puntsog (1922–97), is *Eliminating the Darkness of Extremism: A Commentary to "Praise for Dependent Relativity"* (*Rten 'brel bstod pa'i 'grel pa mthar 'dzin mun sel*), in *Blo bzang dgongs rgyan mu tig phreng mdzes deb*, vol. 4 (Mundgod: Drepung Loseling Educational Society, 1995); and the second, by Lobsang Gyatso, is *Essence of the Sun: Commentary to "The Essence of Eloquence, Praise of Profound Dependent Arising"* (*Rten 'byung gi bstod pa legs par bshad pa'i snying po'i 'grel pa rnam bshad nyi ma'i snying po*) (Dharamsala: Institute of Buddhist Dialectics, 1989). Variant readings in the several versions of the verses I consulted were extremely few. One is noted in commentary on the first verse.

An earlier version of my translation of Tsongkhapa's poem first appeared in *Dreloma*, the magazine of Drepung Loseling Monastic College, and an earlier version of the commentary was published by the Library of Tibetan Works and Archives as *The Harmony of Emptiness and Dependent Arising*. The original lectures on Tsongkhapa's text by Lobsang Gyatso were translated by Sherab Gyatso and transcribed by Effie Hanchett.

Many thanks to all the many others who helped with this book. I would especially like to thank editors Janna White and David Kittelstrom. Finally I would like to express a great debt of gratitude to Geshe Damchoe Gyaltsen, present principal of the Institute of Buddhist Dialectics, my patient teacher over long years of study, seeking the Middle Way view.

Geshe Graham Woodhouse

Praise for Dependent Relativity

Je Tsongkhapa

Namo Guru Manjughoshaya.

1   Through what you realized and proclaimed,
the foremost knower and guide, Subduer,
I bow to you who saw and taught
dependent relativity.

2   Whatever troubles of this world,
their root is ignorance. You taught
the insight that reverses it,
dependent relativity.

3   How then would the intelligent
not comprehend this pathway of
dependent relativity
to be your teaching's very core?

4   In such a case then, no one could
find anything more wonderful
to praise you for than setting forth
dependently arising, Lord.

5   "What on conditions does rely
is empty of inherent being."

What way of fine instruction more
astounding than this utterance?

6   Fools' grasping at it fastens tight
their fetters of extremism.
The same for wise ones is the means
to sever fabrication's net.

7   No others with this teaching seen,
so you alone we Teacher name.
False praise to call a forder that
or give a fox the name of lion.

8   O wondrous teacher, refuge too!
O wondrous speaker, guardian!
I bow to you who taught so well
dependent relativity.

9   Our benefactor, voidness is
the essence of the teachings that
you gave for wandering beings' sake,
dependent relativity

10   The peerless reason proving that.
What way for those to grasp your view
who see it either as unproved
or contradictory? You said

11   Once voidness is perceived as what
arising in dependence means,
then voidness of inherent being
and act and agent harmonize

12   Not contradict. If seen reversed,
the void not fit to act, and on

what acts no voidness, then you said
one plunges to a dread abyss.

13 From what you taught, praise most you saw
arising in dependence then,
for that the nihilists can't see
nor holders to inherent being.

14 The nonreliant are sky flowers,
thus nondependence but a naught.
Establishment by essence blocks
reliance on condition or cause.

15 You taught thus only objects that
dependently arise exist—
thereby no objects save those that
are empty of inherent being.

16 Inherent being has no reverse,
you taught. So, if things had such being,
nirvana could not happen nor
could fabrications be reversed.

17 "Thus, absence of inherent being!"
Within the councils of the wise,
but who could face this lion's roar
repeatedly resounding forth?

18 "Dependent on this, this occurs":
All versions of this well accord
with not the least inherent being.
What need to say they do not clash?

19 "Arising in dependence then
is cause for no dependence on

extremist views." For these fine words
your speech is unexcelled, O Lord.

20 "These all are void of essence" and
"From this arises this effect":
These two discernments mutually
are not opposed, for each helps each.

21 What is there more astonishing
and what more wonderful than this?
So praising you on this account
is praise indeed; no other is.

22 That those who nurse ill will for you,
as slaves of ignorance, should find
the sound of "no inherent being"
unbearable is no surprise.

23 Arising in dependence being
most treasured of your speech, when some
accept it but can't bear the call
of voidness—then I am surprised.

24 Best door to no inherent being,
dependent relativity:
Those nominally for it but
who grasp at *its* inherent being,

25 Well, how can they be led toward
the peerless gates through which progressed
the excellent superior beings,
the noble path that pleases you?

26 Inherent being does not rely
and is unmade. The relative

relies, is made; upon one base,
how do these not just contradict?

27   What things dependently arise,
thereby though free forever from
inherent being, appear that way,
all like illusions then, you said.

28   By this we also properly
may hold to the conclusion that
no disputant, on genuine grounds,
can challenge anything you taught.

29   And why? Because by teaching this
you render distant any chance
to reify or deprecate
unseen or seen phenomena.

30   Arising in dependence is
that path for which your speech is seen
as peerless. It gives certainty
all else you taught is valid too.

31   You saw things as they are and taught
that well. Your students' troubles then
will all recede away, since they
will halt all defects at the root.

32   Who turn away from what you taught
may long perform austerities,
yet they, fixated on the self,
just summon faults repeatedly.

33   Amazing when the wise perceive
the difference between these two.

Then from the very marrow shall
they not have reverence for you?

34 How much you taught, why speak of that?
Determining but generally
the meaning of a single part
just that bestows a special joy.

35 Confusion seized my mind, alas.
Though taking refuge for so long
in that array of qualities,
no part of one have I attained.

36 But while life's stream has not yet sunk
inside the mouth of death itself,
I count it fortunate to have
belief in you, however slight.

37 Of teaching, that of relativity,
of insight, insight into that: these two
are like a great subduer, throughout the worlds
supreme. You saw this well; no others did.

—⁎—

38 All that you taught starts and proceeds
from relativity alone,
and with nirvana as the goal,
no deed of yours was not for peace.

—⁎—

39 Amazing that your teachings bring
all those whose ears they reach to peace,
so who will not hold in esteem
the preservation of your word?

40   All opposition it destroys;
      no contradiction found within.
      It yields all creatures' dual aims.
      My pleasure in this system grows.

41   For countless ages for its sake
      you gave away repeatedly
      at times your body or your life,
      the ones you loved, a mass of wealth.

42   And when you saw its qualities,
      this doctrine drew your heart, as does
      a hook a fish. Sad fate for me
      not hearing it from you yourself.

43   In virtue of this sorrow's strength,
      just like a mother's mind that is
      intent upon a darling child,
      may my mind never deviate.

44   And, dwelling on your speech, I think
      of you, O Teacher, blazing with
      the glories of the signs and marks,
      enhaloed by a radiant light,

45   In your sweet voice discoursing thus
      and thus. As moon rays, fever's pangs,
      O Sage, your likeness brings relief
      in just appearing to my mind.

46   So marvelous and excellent
      a system this, yet those who had
      no mastery, like *balbaja*,
      were tangled up in every way.

47 I recognized their plight and so
I followed in the masters' steps
and your intended meaning sought
repeatedly with greatest zeal.

48 I studied many texts, our own
and those of others, at this time.
My mind was yet repeatedly
all baffled in a net of doubts.

49 When through the lama's kindness I
beheld the grove of all the texts
of Nagarjun, foretold to show
just how your highest vehicle shuns

50 The extremes of being and nonbeing both,
made bloom by white light-garlands of
the speech of glorious Moon, whose sphere
waxed full of stainless wisdom sails

51 Unchecked the heaven of sacred speech,
dispels the heart's extremist gloom,
outshines the stars of erring talk,
O then my mind arrived at rest.

52 Of all the deeds, the deed of speech
was best; of that, of this, and so,
with this your reason, learned ones,
remember the Enlightened One.

—⚬—

53 As follower of this teacher I went forth,
and not ill versed in the Subduer's speech,
I strove in yoga practice as a monk,
such my devotion for that mighty seer.

54   The kindness of the lama brought me to
the foremost teacher's teachings, so too I
this virtue dedicate as cause that all
be cared for by a holy spiritual friend.

55   Our Helper's teachings till the world's end be
not shaken by the wind of evil thoughts,
and be it ever full with those who find
trust in the Teacher, knowing what he taught.

56   May we, no moment's faltering, all our births,
though life or body be the cost, maintain
dependently arising's suchness, this,
the noble way the Sage made manifest.

57   The best of guides, through countless trials, stressed this
to be the essence and let day and night
pass in examining whatever ways
by which what he achieved can be increased.

58   Who strive this way with pure and high resolve,
you, Brahma, Indra, worldly guardians and
protectors, Mahakala and the like,
without distraction always lend your aid.

Colophon

The Essence of Eloquence, Praise to the Supramundane Victor Buddha, Great Friend without Acquaintance to All the World, Foremost Teacher, for Teaching Profound Dependent Relativity was composed by Venerable Losang Dragpa, a monk who has heard many teachings, at Lhading, also called Nampar Gyalway Ling, at the hermitage of Lhashöl, "Beneath the Gods," of Oday Gungyal, mighty among the snowy peaks of the Land of Snows. The scribe was Namkha Pal.

Introduction

T SONGKHAPA, the author of *Praise for Dependent Relativity*, is renowned as one of the greatest scholar-saints that Tibet has ever produced. He composed these verses on the very morning that he abandoned perplexity and attained the final view. In them, he identifies the essence of this view as the harmony of dependent relativity and emptiness. He would later delineate it with fine precision and logical coherence in five great, longer, prose works that are a significant component, if not the core, of his enduring legacy.

Tsongkhapa was born in 1357 in the Tsongkha district of Amdo in northeast Tibet, where Kumbum Monastery now stands. From childhood, his life was wholly devoted to the study and contemplation of Buddha's words, and early animated by the bodhisattva ideal, he strove only for the fully evolved stage of buddhahood, with the vast motivation of helping all beings find freedom. He began his monastic education at the age of three, and he left his home province at the age of sixteen to seek teachings from the masters of central Tibet in the peripatetic style of the times, not restricting himself to any one school or tradition but engaging with many. It was not long before he was called on to teach himself.

His skill in debating and teaching soon brought him fame, but eventually, in 1392, the wisdom-deity Manjushri, with whom Tsongkhapa had established a direct visionary connection, advised him to withdraw from extensive teaching and spend more time in contemplation and retreat.

Tsongkhapa's long years of concentrated study, dedication to the teachings, and arduous practice culminated one night in 1398 when he dreamed that he was present at a discussion of the intricacies of the ultimate view between the most illustrious Buddhist masters of the past. One of them, Buddhapalita, whose commentary Tsongkhapa had been reading the previous evening, approached and blessed him by touching him on the head with a text. Thereupon Tsongkhapa awoke and turned again to Buddhapalita's commentary. As dawn was breaking, he finally generated the blissful, sun-like wisdom that knows the ultimate nature of things and will dispel forever the darkness of ignorance. He composed *Praise for Dependent Relativity* on the same morning, directly following his experience.

Between 1398 and his death, Tsongkhapa devoted his energies to the advancement of Buddhism in Tibet, teaching, composing texts, and founding monasteries. Many of these monasteries, such as the renowned Ganden Monastery, where Tsongkhapa passed away in 1419, have flourished up to the present day as great centers of learning and debate, though now reestablished in exile in India.

One of the remarkable events surrounding Tsongkhapa's life is attested to by two French Christian priests of the Lazarist sect, Huc and Gabet, whose evangelical zeal brought them to Tsongkhapa's birthplace in 1845, a time when very few Westerners had penetrated that isolated region on the eastern edge of the Tibetan plateau. From the earth where the afterbirth expelled from the womb of Tsongkhapa's mother was buried, a tree sprang up with Tibetan letters inscribed on its leaves and bark. The two French missionaries dreamed of preaching the Christian gospel in Lhasa itself. While on their long and adventurous journey from China through Mongolia (Tartary) to the Tibetan capital, they stopped to recuperate for a few weeks at Kumbum Monastery. By way of preface to their description of the tree that they had already heard so much about on their travels, their antipathy to the Buddhist religion is worth noticing. In Mongolia, Huc confides:

> Sad and lamentable is it to see these unhappy victims of error...; one's heart is pierced with grief, and one's soul impressed with yearning for the day when these poor Tartars

shall consecrate to the service of the true God that religious energy which they daily waste upon a vain and lying creed.[1]

Not long after arriving Kumbum, Huc and Gabet passed through the gate of the wall enclosing the renowned tree:

> Our eyes were first directed with earnest curiosity to the leaves, and we were filled with an absolute consternation of astonishment at finding that, in point of fact, there were upon each of the leaves well-formed Thibetian characters, all of a green color, some darker, some lighter than the leaf itself. Our first impression was a suspicion of fraud on the part of the Lamas; but, after a minute examination of every detail, we could not discover the least deception. The characters all appeared to us portions of the leaf itself, equally with its veins and nerves; the position was not the same in all; in one leaf they would be at the top of the leaf; in another, in the middle; in a third, at the base, or at the side; the younger leaves represented the characters only in a partial state of formation. The bark of the tree and its branches, which resemble that of the plane tree, are also covered with these characters. When you remove a piece of old bark, the young bark under it exhibits the indistinct outlines of characters in a germinating state, and, what is very singular, these new characters are not infrequently different from those which they replace. We examined everything with the closest attention, in order to detect some trace of trickery, but we could discern nothing of the sort, and the perspiration absolutely trickled down our faces under the influence of the sensations which this most amazing spectacle created. More profound intellects than ours may, perhaps, be able to supply a satisfactory explanation of the mysteries of his singular tree; but as to us, we altogether give it up. Our readers possibly may smile at our ignorance; but we care not, so that the sincerity and truth of our statement be not suspected.[2]

The vitality of Tsongkhapa's influence, the distinctiveness of his philosophical interpretations, and the popularity of his style of practice were so great that his followers soon became numerous enough to be identified as the fourth and latest major grouping within Tibetan Buddhism, eventually distinguished from the Nyingmapas, the Kagyupas, and the Sakyapas as the Gelug sect. Foremost among the masters of the Gelugpas has been the distinguished line of fourteen Dalai Lamas, the first of whom, Gendun Drub (1391–1474), was one of Tsongkhapa's direct disciples. No more need be said to show how enormous and far-reaching Tsongkhapa's influence on Tibet's religious and secular affairs has been.

Today the central, essential meaning of *Praise for Dependent Relativity* is as vital as ever. A deeper understanding, where the heart is at rest, emerges from clearly appreciating the dependently related nature of things. It undercuts the arrogance of the powerful and the narrow-minded. It eradicates the despair and insecurity of those who are unable to connect. Here at last the self is revealed in its true colors, and the distorted self-importance and self-obsession that hurt us more than anything in the world drop away.

Buddha taught that, with the deepest understanding of dependent relativity, there is, if we wish, a passing away from travail, a complete suspension of the burden of involvement in a world such as this, whose very fabric is spun from delusion. For more ardent natures, those who erase all vestiges of self-concern whatsoever, there is the bodhisattva's striving for evolution's highest stage, buddhahood, and his or her willing acceptance of involvement in such afflicted worlds as this one, helping where help is needed until all beings have happiness.

For the Buddhist, dependent relativity is at the heart of all true paths, but we need not be Buddhists to respond to the message of dependent relativity and to derive inspiration from it. Arguments establishing it stand or fall on clear-cut and logical grounds. Buddhist or non-Buddhist, anyone's practical steps in daily affairs will become firmer and gentler when taken in full awareness of the basic dependent nature of all we encounter.

A few steps further down the road, perhaps we will open to our first glimpse of that which Tsongkhapa gazed upon in serenity on the morning he composed these stanzas: the furthest implication of dependent relativity, ultimate reality, emptiness, the mysterious and liberating truth that nothing has any intrinsic nature whatsoever.

1. Victorious

Praise for Dependent Relativity is Tsongkhapa's spontaneous outpouring of devotion to Shakyamuni Buddha for his teachings, especially the revelation of the essence of wisdom that had just dawned in Tsongkhapa's mind. The text is an expression of the author's redoubled faith in Buddha. Its eloquence inspires curiosity and faith in others, drawing them into the study and practice of these teachings and setting them in turn on the path that leads to freedom. Tsongkhapa writes with a sense of fulfillment and a certainty of the truth of these teachings. Thus assured, he turns his mind completely toward the welfare of others.

Buddha's teaching, the Dharma, is not merely a pleasant diversion but rather a powerful medicine. Buddha showed how the deep cause of all suffering lies within, ultimately tracing it back to afflicted or deluded states of mind. He showed that turbulent emotions such as jealousy, hatred, attachment, and ignorant fanaticism are responsible for the harmful actions we do and, directly or indirectly, these actions bring about all the suffering of the world.

Dharma teachings are designed to nourish the mind and bring about restrained and balanced attitudes of equanimity and compassion so that we can remain content whatever the external conditions. Then, with the powerful sword of wisdom, we can sever the very root of all delusions, mental afflictions, and negative emotions and thereby completely emancipate ourselves from dissatisfaction. Even Buddha, whose knowledge is unlimited, was once a human being and began by relying on the encouragement and teachings of others. The same way is now open to us. If the teacher can teach and the student can listen in this spirit, putting away all thoughts of fame, praise, material gain, or worldly knowledge, great benefit can ensue.

The five prose works that Tsongkhapa composed on the view of emptiness contain a thorough evaluation of the many contrasting interpretations of Buddha's teachings on the profound view that arose in the centuries after his passing away. *Praise for Dependent Relativity* presents, as we will see, the very essence of this issue, so it is an excellent introduction to the main philosophic question on the path to liberation: What did Buddha mean when he taught selflessness or emptiness?

In *Praise for Dependent Relativity* Tsongkhapa could not be more pointed in emphasizing the equivalence of emptiness and dependent relativity. In stressing this, he makes no claim to originality. He might have said that his elucidation was only a tweak of interpretation to bring Buddha's intended meaning back into focus, but in the face of so many wayward assertions, it is a much needed tweak and an utterly crucial one. With an understanding of this equivalence, the sword of wisdom is tempered and sharp. Without it, there is no cutting through. Making this one point crystal clear is the philosophical agenda of these verses.

Namo Guru Manjughoshaya.

First Tsongkhapa pays reverence to his guru, Manjughosha, or Manjushri, seeking inspiration for the composition of his text.

1   Through what you realized and proclaimed,
the foremost knower and guide, Subduer,
I bow to you who saw and taught
dependent relativity.[3]

In the first verse, Tsongkhapa singles out Buddha's powers of wisdom and speech, especially his insight into and revelation of dependent relativity. Buddha perfected his own understanding of dependent relativity and then taught it widely, thoroughly elucidating its far-reaching implications. He is supreme for these qualities. They are the source of his mastery. Tsongkhapa begins by bowing low to the one who is distinguished by these accomplishments.

Buddha had an outstanding ability to teach in accordance with his listeners' predispositions and needs. Through the completeness of his knowledge—indeed, his omniscience—he understood each individual listener's capacities and inclinations and skillfully taught according to their levels of understanding. For instance, as we will see, his teaching on selflessness has several different levels, each helpful for a certain type of person at a certain stage of development. Simpler presentations are superseded by more refined and subtle explanations until Buddha's final view becomes clear.

Buddha's teachings are not the kind of teachings that are attractive and pleasant to listen to but unable to bear reasoned analysis. The ability to withstand that kind of scrutiny is a distinguishing feature of Buddha's message of liberation. All religions present a path to lasting happiness, but the authenticity of Buddha's path does not depend on intuition, divine revelation, or dogmatic authority. The resultant state of happiness is not achieved by appeasing a potentially harmful power or bestowed by a ruling deity. Rather, freedom comes when we remove the defilements of ignorance from our own minds. We do this by cultivating reason-based wisdom and then through concentrated meditation on the insights that wisdom brings.

Buddha has many marvelous qualities, and faith in such a being yields an abundance of good effects. The best possible basis for such faith is not merely to believe out of awe and admiration that he shows an authentic way to end suffering but to establish it with reasoning. The stages of the path (*lamrim*) guidebooks arrange Buddha's many teachings into a clear sequence of mental development. We must think through the understandings set out there and take them to heart one by one. Prayer and other forms of devotion certainly help to make the mind supple, removing dullness and awakening the pure energy necessary to make these insights our own. But the Buddha's exposition of dependent relativity and its corollary, emptiness, is thoroughly amenable to plain logical analysis. These twin truths are indeed the key insight in dependence on which Buddha became the triumphant "Subduer," as Tsongkhapa praises him in the first verse.

Buddha is called a Subduer, or Conqueror, because he has finally, completely, and irreversibly vanquished the two obstructions and the four *maras*. The *two obstructions* are the obstructions of the afflictions and the obstructions to omniscience. The *obstructions of the afflictions* are the mental defilements that prevent us from attaining personal liberation. By mental defilements we mean the negative states of mind mentioned earlier: ignorant and destructive views, especially of the nature of the self; possessiveness; greed; hatred; and the like. Personal liberation is nirvana, a stable state of withdrawal and peace where suffering and conflict are at last extinct and one is free of any compulsion to take rebirth. The second set of obstructions, the *obstructions to omniscience*, are the subtler defilements that prevent us from attaining the unlimited, direct understanding and the all-embracing compassion of a buddha. The removal of these obstructions requires many more lifetimes of striving, not simply to fulfill our own longing for peace but to achieve a vast, enlightened capacity to free masses of others from dissatisfaction and bewilderment also.

Mara means demon, or demonic influence, that hinders the practice of virtue. It may be an external spirit or an aspect of our own imperfect condition. All hindrances on the path to liberation are subsumed under the *four maras*. The first mara is the *mara of the aggregates*. Our aggregates are the parts that make us up—our body and mind. Many of us, being relatively free of illness or injury, have a body that offers great opportunities. But despite our constant attempts to cherish it and attend to its every whim, having such a body also renders us vulnerable to the sufferings of hunger, thirst, heat, cold, illness, and old age. Since our aggregates cannot be depended on and hinder our progress in so many ways, their unsatisfactory aspect is given the name *mara*.

The second of the maras is the *mara of the afflictions*, which are the same as the afflictive obstructions. They are identified as a mara because they precipitate all harmful actions, from malicious gossip to murder. Unlike the suffering inflicted by an external enemy, which lasts for a maximum of one lifetime, the seeds of the afflictions, unless we do something about them, stay in our minds and accompany us from life to life, ever ready to manifest. All forms of conflict can be traced back to this internal demon: the conflicts between nations, within a community, between members of a family, right down to the fighting and bickering that goes on between small children.

The third mara is Devaputra, literally "son of a god," an external troublemaker who specializes in interfering with beings who are endeavoring to achieve something positive. There are many entertaining stories of his attempts to outwit Buddha in his progress as a bodhisattva. According to another explanation, this mara personifies the temptations of alluring desire.

The last mara is the *mara of death*. Death is sometimes portrayed a particular being, the Lord of Death, but this is simply a projection. What is intended here is the fact that we have to die soon enough, without knowing when and without the power to postpone it for a second. This great interrupter of life's hopes and aspirations is the fourth hindrance that Buddha completely overcame in order to reach full enlightenment.

The enlightenment of a subduer is an exalted state. When we overcome the two obstructions and the four maras we reach the highest level of mental evolution, where there are no longer any obstacles to complete knowing and universal compassion. We can only achieve that state through a great series of lifetimes spent in the practice of both wisdom and altruism. It is the end of our time as a limited being, the stage when we achieve our full potential to benefit others, not least as guides on the same transcendent path.

2. The Root of All Troubles

2   Whatever troubles of this world,
    their root is ignorance. You taught
    the insight that reverses it,
    dependent relativity.

ALL CREATURES ARE engaged in seeking happiness and trying to avoid suffering. For those of us who are aware of how precariously we balance between happiness and sorrow, and who have sufficient leisure to ponder our predicament, Tsongkhapa recommends Buddha's teaching of dependent relativity or dependent arising. All things arise in dependence on phenomena other than themselves. At the simplest level, all things and all situations arise in dependence on causes and conditions. Of course, this is not exactly news to us, but that's exactly what we forget when some unexpected incident propels us into frustration or annoyance. It happens when the milk boils over even though we thought we were being so watchful. Would we get so irritated if we were more conscious of the play of forces at work?

When someone lets us down by being late for a rendezvous, annoyance starts simmering inside us (though it does not warm our hands and feet if we are kept standing in the cold!). However, as soon as the real cause for that person's delay is understood, the anger and impatience begin to subside. There is often a sound reason, and knowing it smoothes away our vexation. If there is no good reason, he is simply a hopeless case, and why should we let hopeless cases ruffle us? A wrathful appearance may be useful to coerce the lazy or unwilling, but it should not be accompanied by actual bitterness or hostility, or spring from an elevated sense of our own importance. Some people may think letting out their anger at others is a good thing, but being angry is uncomfortable. It distorts our judgment, and it triggers hot and hasty actions, exaggerating our sense of injury. There is a Tibetan proverb that says, "Be careful what you say: spit and harsh words cannot be taken back."

How we react to being let down also depends a great deal on how the other party appears to our mind. He is not in and of himself the stimulus for our anger. It depends not on him alone but on factors personal to us: how fond we are of him, how tired we are, the mood we are in, our culturally induced expectations of punctuality, and so forth.

An object's dependence on causes and conditions and its dependence on the viewpoint of the observer are just a couple of the relationships included in the term *dependent relativity*. A deep acquaintance with these factors—which can be gained through meditation—will help us to handle our own temper and others' unreliability with confidence.

So thoroughgoing is the dependently related nature of all phenomena that in fact nothing has any inherent, intrinsic, or independent nature whatsoever. This is what we mean by the *emptiness of inherent existence* (Skt. *svabhava-shunyata*). When we realize dependent relativity at this deeper level, we will then be in a position to abandon its opposite—the instinctive, distorted view that all phenomena are inherently existent, which Buddha identified as the ignorance that is the root of all troubles. As Tsongkhapa explains, without understanding dependent relativity at a profound level, we cannot arrive at the ultimate view of emptiness. Without familiarizing ourselves again and again with the ultimate view, we cannot destroy the root ignorance. Without destroying this ignorance, we can never find release from the sufferings of the world, nor can we go beyond that deliverance to attain the beneficial potential of a fully enlightened being. Hence it is utterly essential to understand dependent relativity and emptiness exactly as Buddha intended.

However, the Buddhist sutras contain a variety of treatments of this central issue. As we explore the controversies concerning these different explanations, the mutual dependence of causes and effects, parts and wholes, generalities and instances, self and others, and subject and object will become clear. And all those forms of dependent relationships will have to be reinterpreted in light of the most subtle aspect of dependent relativity—the fact that all phenomena are mere designations upon a basis of designation by a designating consciousness.

Given the diverging interpretations of dependent relativity and selflessness codified in the tenets of various schools of Buddhist thought, we would be extremely fortunate to find a teacher who could explain dependent relativity flawlessly. Thus our way to proceed should be to bring together the teachings of living masters with our own analysis and study of Buddhist texts.

However, before we delve into all the different versions of dependent relativity, we first have to justify the diagnosis that ignorance is indeed the root of "whatever troubles of this world."

Many of us pass our whole lives in the pursuit of temporary forms of fulfillment, doubtful that there is any such thing as a lasting state of happiness where all troubles are finally abandoned. Such people may well suppose that suffering in the form of old age, sickness, and death is unavoidable. To such questions as "What are we here for?" "Why is there dissatisfaction?" and "Why does my innocent child have to go through this ordeal?" their answer is that, in the face of a mystery, man's lot is perplexity.

The outlook of many Westerners today is basically materialist, where one looks to describe the whole of life, including the mind, in physical terms. From that perspective, these questions may indeed seem hard to penetrate. Buddhism's response is that the mind is a nonmaterial phenomenon that cannot arise out of the interactions of a conglomeration of material particles that are themselves individually insentient. The only possible substantial cause for a moment of mind is a previous moment of that continuum of mind. By *substantial cause* we mean a cause whose continuum passes into the effect. A seed is the substantial cause of its effect, a sprout, but a potter is not the substantial cause of a clay pot. In this way, an individual's mind has experienced many previous lives before inhabiting the present body. This process of reincarnation will go on until liberation is achieved.

In explaining the ways of the world, the universe, and life, Buddhism acknowledges the primacy of mind over matter. The kind of world we are thrown into at birth, and points on the spectrum of happiness and unhappiness we will touch as we wander there, depend to a significant extent on our actions in previous lives. In other words, we reap what we sow. Many people have an intuitive feeling that this is the case, that the evil we do will come back to haunt us and that the good we do will lift us up. The Buddhist portrayal of life based on the three components—the nonmateriality of mind, karma, and rebirth—shows how such a process of balancing out takes place. Thus these three factors must be the starting point for any incisive response to the above perennial questions. We will base our investigation of this response on Buddha's teachings of the four truths and the twelve links of dependent relativity.

The Four Truths

If a person falls ill, in order to treat him and make him well, the doctor must first take careful note of the symptoms of the disease and, from them, determine its root causes. Administering a medicine that merely relieves the symptoms is insufficient; the patient wants a remedy that will eradicate the disease and bring him back to sound health. So the doctor makes a diagnosis and then prescribes a course of treatment that will get rid of the problem. The patient follows the doctor's instructions and is cured.

This analogy serves well to introduce Buddha's basic teaching of the four truths. We are the patient and our condition is known as true suffering, which is the first of the four truths. The causes of our disease are true origins, the second of the truths. The state of health we hope to achieve corresponds to the third truth, true cessation. And the course of treatment that brings about the desired state of health is equivalent to the fourth truth, true paths.

True suffering refers to all the troubles we face, all the sorrow, loss, and pain we encounter in this round of existence. However exalted our worldly status, we all have to stand naked before physical anguish and mental anxiety. We do not escape the pangs of birth, aging, sickness, and death. Not only that, we never seem to be satisfied. We may have what we need, but we always crave more. If we get what we desire, we hanker after something else. The very things that give us pleasure become unpleasant if indulged in too much, like when we overeat or sit in the sun too long. Even if we are happy at a certain moment, we have to acknowledge the unsatisfactory reality that, sooner or later, we are bound to undergo suffering again.

The troubles of this world are easy to enumerate at length. The challenge is identifying their ultimate source, like the doctor's diagnosing the root cause of the patient's illness. True origins, or the causes of true suffering, are of two types—karma and mental afflictions. The first, karma or action, arises in dependence upon the second, the afflictions, since our acts are set in motion by our mental inclinations. The five main afflictions, known as the *five poisons*, are: attachment, anger, ignorance, pride, and envy.

The third truth is true cessations. Just like the state of freedom after overcoming a disease, we are guaranteed the liberation that is the final abandonment of suffering when we have the complete collection of true cessations. The true cessations are the abandonment of all the mental afflictions such that they will never arise to distort our mind again. The last of the truths, true paths, likened to the course of treatment the patient undergoes, are the realizations and the wisdom that counteract the mental afflictions. Those who achieve liberation do so by generating this wisdom and meditating deeply on it. That is the method to erase all the afflictions and their seeds.

Returning to the second truth, true origins, we can illustrate how ignorance is the root of all suffering with the example of the act of killing. In this context, the ignorance of dependent arising has two main aspects—ignorance of karma and ignorance of selflessness. The ignorance concerning the workings of karma is described first.

Some people hunt or fish for sport and regard killing as a pastime. Others operate slaughterhouses or commercial fishing boats and feel satisfaction at killing, thinking of the profit they will obtain from selling the flesh of their victims. For such people, the apparent effect of killing is happiness. They deliberately engage in the action in the expectation of pleasure. It may well be that in the short term their expectations are fulfilled—the hunter feeds himself or enjoys his trophy, and the butcher counts his profits.

However, the long-term effects of these actions are far from pleasurable. According to the principles of karma, actions are never wasted. Unless purified, they are sure to produce miserable consequences for the doer, possibly later in this life, more often in a future life. One who kills will experience suffering proportionate to the suffering he inflicted and the degree of enthusiasm with which he inflicted it. One who commits very harmful actions is liable to take rebirth in a lower state, such as the hells or hungry ghost realms. If the action is less intensely negative, he may take a less unfortunate animal rebirth. Other consequences may also flow from his act of killing. Even if he is born in the human realm, his lifespan may be very short, and he may have the ingrained tendency to enjoy taking others' lives again and again. On the other hand, it is possible to purify negative karma through the appropriate Dharma practices such that none of the above consequences are absolutely certain to occur.

Much also depends on the strength of intention. In our example, we painted a picture of a very deliberate negative motivation. But one can also kill accidentally or reluctantly, without a strongly selfish aim. In these circumstances, the negative action of killing would still be committed, but the ripened effects of the action would be lighter. The way the ripened effects of different actions can blend together is another variable. Here we are referring to what are known as *projecting karma* and *completing karma*. The projecting karma from a previous act of killing might, for instance, throw us into a future life as a dog. But completing karma from another previous positive action might ripen in that same lifetime such that we are sheltered by kind people who provide us with excellent food and other comforts. Similarly, good projecting karma can bring about a higher state of rebirth, only to be complemented by miserable completing karma.

In the end, all the pleasure we experience comes about due to the virtuous actions we commit, the actions that benefit others; all the suffering we experience comes about due to the nonvirtuous and harmful actions we accumulate. In our example, the butcher is heedless of the cruelty of his actions and oblivious to their long-term karmic effects. He snatches at the precarious satisfactions of this life, only to be whirled again and again into the sufferings of the transitory round of existence, a leaf blown by the wind of karma.

It is crucial for us to contemplate this aspect of dependent relativity very carefully and gain conviction concerning the principles of karma. If we do so, it will help us to decide once and for all to stop taking life—the firmer the decision, the better. A much greater benefit arises when we actively determine not to kill than when we merely happen not to do so. The former is a fully fledged wholesome action whose ripening effect will be happiness.

If the action of determining to abandon killing ripened up at death, that virtuous action would lead to rebirth in one of the fortunate realms, such as in the human realm with a precious spark of intelligence and self-awareness, or in a realm of more guaranteed happiness. It could be in a godlike realm, where pain is completely absent and we enjoy again and again the pleasures of refined sense-gratification.

Here we get a glimpse of the cosmos as depicted in Buddhist terms. The myriad worlds beyond our own are differentiated from ours primarily in terms of what levels of pleasure or suffering are encountered there. In a universe vast beyond imagining, there can be found the whole spectrum, from states of unbearable hellish torture, mental alienation, and derangement, to the states of exalted, expansive, meditative tranquility where the clog of gross matter has long been transcended. But even those born in divine worldly realms do not escape suffering for good; they have not overcome the mara of death. However luxuriously or serenely long their lives, in due course, their happiness too comes to an end. They experience the trauma of death again and migrate to another life and yet another.

A person who has some understanding of karma and strives to refrain from harmful acts like killing thereby improves her chances of happiness. But if she is still ensnared by the second ignorance, the ignorance concerning the ultimate nature of self and phenomena, then her hopes will remain limited to favorable experiences within cyclic existence. By contrast, there is the person who, with some understanding of selflessness or emptiness, develops a pure and powerful wish to take control and free herself from the unsatisfactory round of death and rebirth driven by delusion and unskillful action.

The clarity of the insight Tsongkhapa attained on the morning he composed his verses is such that the ignorance that provokes us again and again into misery cannot abide simultaneously with it. In its presence, the mistaken ignorance gives way, just as the darkness in a room vanishes when we turn on the light. For somebody who has recognized the power of such wisdom and has thereby generated an authentic determination to forsake cyclic existence, the action of decisively refraining from killing ripens in accordance with this strong wish. It brings us closer to liberation.

Abandoning killing in the hope of gaining release from the wheel of existence is still not the highest motivation we can aspire to. We can abandon killing such that the karma ripens up as some form of pleasure within the round of existence. Beyond that, we can abandon killing as part of our efforts to gain our own individual complete liberation from that round. But best of all is to abandon killing with the pure wish to be of the utmost benefit to as many sentient beings as possible.

We dwell on the fact that suffering descends not just on us but on all alike, and we contemplate that a buddha is the one who has the highest wisdom and most skillful means to separate beings from their suffering. Thus we develop the ever-arising, spontaneous resolve to become a buddha for the benefit of all. This aspiration is called *bodhicitta*, or the mind of enlightenment. The one who has it is a *bodhisattva*. When coupled with the precious bodhicitta in this way, the virtuous action of decisively abandoning killing contributes to our development toward buddhahood. Buddhahood is the highest form of enlightenment because it is not for ourselves alone but for the sake of all sentient beings.

Thus, depending on our motivation, the long-term results of our virtuous actions, such as forsaking harming others or generosity, can either be worldly pleasure, the peace of individual emancipation, or the fulfillment of arriving at the very highest and most beneficial state of mental evolution.

Whether we can develop the higher levels of motivation depends on how obscured our minds are with regard to selflessness, the ultimate nature of self and phenomena. This is the second of the two types of ignorance concerning dependent arising mentioned above. It is not necessary to be like Tsongkhapa and to have developed the actual wisdom of the ultimate view in order to be able to accumulate actions that contribute to our attainment of nirvana or buddhahood. But the minimum we need is an appropriate, strong, well-informed motivation accompanying our positive deeds. When we visualize the buddhas collectively in front of us, they are known as the *field of merit*. The power of this field is also a significant factor. Actions such as prostrating to the buddhas or meditating on their inconceivable aspects give rise to effects that go beyond cyclic existence, even if our understanding of the path to freedom is imperfect.

Some call ignorance the creator of the world. Other Buddhist schools say that karma is the creator of the world. The Consequentialists, the school of Buddhist philosophy to which Tsongkhapa belonged, say it is the mind. These explanations are not contradictory. Karma can be likened to the soldiers who perform acts of shooting and killing in a battle, while ignorance can be likened to the president who orders his country's troops to war. We can point our finger at the soldiers and say they did the killing, but we can also say the ultimate responsibility for those acts lies with the president.

In any case, Buddhist thought ultimately traces the causes of the world back to our own minds. No place has been found for a creator-being, an architect, or a prime mover who brings forth the universe of his or her own volition. The source of our problems lies within our own minds, and so does the remedy. This is the import of Buddha's teaching on the four truths.

The Twelve Links of Dependent Relativity

The teaching on the twelve links of dependent relativity portrays the stages of cyclic existence in more detail. The verbal teaching is often accompanied by a vivid depiction of the wheel of existence designed by Buddha himself. It can be seen at the entrance to the prayer halls of most Tibetan monasteries. In the center a pig, a cock, and a snake symbolize the *three poisons*—ignorance, desirous attachment, and hatred—which set the whole round in motion. Outside the center circle, we see karma at work, dragging beings down to misfortune or lifting them up to happier states. The next outer circle shows the six main types of rebirth in cyclic existence, from the hellish realm to the godlike. The twelve links form the outermost circle of the wheel. The twelve links are:

1. Ignorance
2. Compositional karma
3. Consciousness
4. Name and form
5. Six sources
6. Contact
7. Feeling
8. Attachment
9. Grasping
10. Existence
11. Birth
12. Aging and death

An apposite picture illustrates each link. Ignorance is a blind man stumbling along; compositional karma is the shaping of a clay pot on a wheel; and so on. The whole circle is held fast in the menacing embrace of Yama, the lord of death, while an enlightened being stands outside and above, pointing out the way of escape. Much may be said to reveal the pertinent details of this key teaching, but here we will just briefly show how the twelve links might evolve for an individual person over the course of two lifetimes.

The first of the twelve links is ignorance, the distorted grasping at "me" and "mine" as inherently existent that obstructs our awareness of their selfless, dependently arisen nature. Under the influence of this ignorance, the person commits an action, whether positive, negative, or neutral, and this action forms the second link, compositional karma. Until it ripens in a future lifetime or later in this one, this action is stored in the consciousness in the form of a potential or seed. Consciousness is the third link, and it is like the earth in which a seed rests until the other conditions necessary for it to germinate come together. If a seed is to germinate, one condition it certainly needs is moisture. In the case of a karmic seed, the equivalent of moisture is desirous attachment, or attachment to the forms and features of cyclic existence with which one has such an ingrained familiarity. In the sequence of twelve links, attachment is the eighth, and it is to that which we now pass.

The particular attachment referred to here is the attachment that manifests in the mind of someone who is on the verge of death. As death nears, the person's ordinary sense consciousnesses fade, and there arises a strong inclination for a particular type of rebirth, as a certain kind of animal, human, or whatever. The next link, the ninth, grasping, is when that attachment strengthens up. Appearances are said to arise to his mind of the bodily forms or birthplaces that he is attracted to and wants to associate with.

The tenth link is called *existence*, and refers not to the next life itself but to its immediate cause, the fully potentialized karma that throws the person into the next life. This is the compositional karma of the second link in an activated state, energized by conditions such as attachment. The six links we have mentioned so far—the first, second, third, eighth, ninth, and tenth—are a causal sequence. The link of existence is the last moment of that sequence. The connection between the person's body and mind ceases. The consciousness departs from one life and travels on to the next.

The eleventh link in the twelve, and the first of the effect sequence, is birth. However, there is an intermediate stage between the end of one life and the start of another. In this stage, the person has a body of such a subtle form that it is not obstructed by gross matter such as walls, nor is it visible to ordinary eyes. We can think of a radio broadcast being transmitted from the station to the place where someone is listening to the radio. Something travels from the broadcasting station to the receiver. It is not sound; we could say it is the potential to produce sound. The force that causes the radio waves to travel from one place to another is like the fully potentialized karma in the twelve links. When the radio waves reach the receiver, various sounds come forth. Similarly, the force of karma propels a consciousness, together with its very subtle energy body, to a place of conception, where it joins with a body of gross form—the uniting sperm and egg of the father and mother in the case of human and many animal births—and a new creature arises. Strictly speaking, however, the link of birth begins before the process of conception with the adoption of the subtle body of the intermediate stage right after death.

Of all our actions whose effects have not yet worked themselves out, only the one that ripens at death is responsible for determining what category of rebirth we will experience. Why should one particular action and not another ripen at this crucial time? Some actions leave a trace on the mind that is too weak ever to ripen. Others are more liable to ripen because the impression they leave on the mind is sharp and strong. There is also the factor of how familiar we are with a certain action. The more often we have committed an action, the more likely it is that one of that type will ripen at the moment of death and be the one that steers us to our new world.

Next we progress to the fourth link, the link of name and form. The link of name and form begins when the consciousness, or name, joins with its new body, or form. It covers the first stage of embryonic development before the eye, ear, nose, and tongue sense faculties begin to form. The stage of development distinguished by the formation of these sense powers is the fifth link, the link of the six sources. The remaining two of the six sources—the body sense faculty, which enables tactile sensation, and the mental sense faculty—are present from conception onward.

The five physical sense faculties give to their respective consciousnesses—eye consciousness, ear consciousness, and so forth—the ability to be generated in the aspect of and to apprehend their respective objects—visual form, sound, and so forth. The sixth sense faculty, which empowers mental as opposed to sense consciousness, is not physical, but is simply the previous moment of consciousness.

The sixth link is called *contact*. In the contact stage, the sense consciousnesses, beginning with the body consciousness and followed by the ear consciousness, start to have involvement with their objects. The subtle consciousness that entered the womb has given rise to gross levels of consciousness once more, which have their avenues of communication, the sense powers. When the sense consciousnesses make contact with their objects, the seventh link, feeling, occurs.

Aging and death constitute the twelfth and final link. The process of aging has been occurring since birth. Another circuit of the wheel of existence comes to an end when the twelfth link's terminal stage, death, occurs. When life cannot be prolonged any further, the ordinary levels of consciousness of waking life dissolve back into a more subtle state. The mind leaves its old body, stripped of wealth, fame, possessions, loved ones, and family, and heads once more toward the next life.

The twelve links can unfold over the interval of just two lifetimes. In our former life, we created the first three links—ignorance, karma, and consciousness—and also links eight, nine, and ten—desirous attachment, grasping, and existence. These are the six causal links that brought about this life. The remaining links—four, name and form; five, six sources; six, contact; seven, feeling; eleven, birth; and twelve, aging and death—are the six effect links we are now passing through in this life. Only the final link's terminal stage, death, has yet to be completed.

Even now, we are accumulating many different actions all the time. Any action that is strong enough can give rise to a future birth, in the human realm or any other. We are continually creating causes for being reborn. As we are experiencing the six effect links, we are also accumulating the six causal links that will culminate in our next life. Thus it is impossible to point a finger and say, "This is the start of it all."

This beginningless, wandering round is what is called *cyclic existence* or *samsara*. We should meditate repeatedly on it in order to turn decisively away from its superficial enticements. We should familiarize ourselves with the advantages of the peaceful state of liberation and make the wish for everyone to go there our strongest urge. We must probe again and again to identify the distorted grasping that hoodwinks us and confines us here and to discover just what the insight is that shatters it asunder.

3   How then would the intelligent
    not comprehend this pathway of
    dependent relativity
    to be your teaching's very core?

4 In such a case then, no one could
   find anything more wonderful
   to praise you for than setting forth
   dependently arising, Lord.

The mind that understands dependent relativity is itself the "pathway" of verse 3. We generally understand a *path* as a way we traverse to get to our destination. In the present context, it is apt to call the mind that realizes dependent relativity a *path* because cultivating that mind, familiarizing ourselves with it again and again, and dwelling on it in meditation is the way we travel to liberation.

In verse 3 Tsongkhapa singles out the wisdom of dependent relativity for the third time. A glowing reference to "dependent arising" follows in verse 4. Dependent arising is simply dependent relativity by a different name. The rhetorical force of all these repetitions is very powerful. After all, Buddha's most famous teaching is his teaching on selflessness or emptiness—ultimate truth. Is it not supposed to be insight into emptiness that cuts through confusion and bulldozes the prison of cyclic existence?

We should note, however, that the first mention of emptiness does not occur until verse 5. It is as if Tsongkhapa wants to make it clear from the very beginning that the emptiness that is crucial is the emptiness that is the furthest consequence of dependent relativity. Any version of selflessness or emptiness not congruent with the full meaning of dependent relativity—and many have been propounded—is inadequate and in vain. Such an understanding of emptiness is not what makes the Subduer unsurpassed in wisdom, not what dispatches the four maras, not what reverses all causes of suffering, not the very core of the teachings, and not what Buddha deserves to be praised for above all else.

Of guides to the destination of highest happiness, only Buddha reveals dependent arising, unsurpassed in effectiveness, in all its implications. Of Buddhist schools, only the Consequentialists of Tsongkhapa's ilk are able to explain this teaching in all its magnificent depth and clarity. It is to an illumination of these assertions that we now proceed.

3. Cause and Effect

5ab "What on conditions does rely
is empty of inherent being."

ONSIDER HOW we ordinarily apprehend things to exist. Do we
not naturally feel that the self and the everyday objects around
us are established from their own side, that they are each substantial and concrete entities that exist in and of themselves? Think of
how we apprehend ourselves when we are in a perilous situation, such
as when we go near the edge of a steep cliff. Clutched by fear, do we
not appear to ourselves to exist independently, simply by our own
power? All of our perceptions are tinged with this type of appearance.
When we glance at a watch, for example, does it not seem to have its
own independent, self-sufficient nature, over and above any relationships that exist between it and other phenomena?

Many schools of thought, non-Buddhist and Buddhist, and Eastern
and Western, display tremendous ingenuity in how they attend to the
challenge of explaining how things arise in reliance upon various conditions, i.e., causes. Most of these schools assume that things do inherently exist. According to the Consequentialists, however, this perception
is false. Because all phenomena arise in dependence on conditions, they
cannot be inherently existent at all. The truth of the matter is that things
are not established from their own side and do not exist by way of their
own power. Understanding this precisely and thoroughly is the way to
depart from all the troubles of this transitory world.

This understanding is also vital to the present, to our everyday lives.
We may check to see whether the claim is true that whenever we are

thrown off balance by a negative emotion such as attachment, envy, impatience, or rage, the reaction is always triggered by a moment of false grasping. Your computer suddenly twitches, you lose a bundle of precious data, and your anger comes blazing forth. But just concentrate on the very first moment of the sequence of your negative reaction. Did you not, in that instant, entirely forget the web of causes and conditions and apprehend yourself and your computer to exist completely by their own power? What brings you back down to earth is the recollection of that web of causes and conditions. You think, "Oh yes, I forgot to save the document." It is only an imperfect machine, after all.

The greatest regard is due to all those religions, paths of practice, and systems of knowledge that inspire people to live in the better halves of themselves and contribute to the welfare of others. The following few remarks, intended to bring out the broad principles of Buddhist thought by contrasting them with other ideas, are therefore in no way intended to disparage anybody else's convictions, religious or otherwise. Disagreement with others' views should not be taken to imply any lack of tolerance or respect. Intolerance is when one is not allowed to disagree.

Many traditions accept that the world was created by God, and God's existence is not generally understood to be under the influence of causes and conditions. If the origin of God is discussed at all, the consensus seems to be that he or she is eternal or self-created, abiding beyond fluctuation and instability. These types of traditions point to cause-and-effect relationships when trying to explain how things came about and how they exist. Tracing the causes backward, they arrive at a primordial being who stands outside the realm of change, an ultimate source from which all other phenomena derive their inherently existent natures.

Some schools that accept reincarnation view the concept of "I" or "self" in a similar fashion. According to their reasoning, we observe ourselves reading, eating, and working, and, tracing these actions back to their source, we arrive at the self—it is the I that causes these actions to be performed. The source of our actions, they argue, has to be something substantial and truly existent, even unchanging. If the I is forever changing, how can we speak of any identity that goes from one life to the next? Amid the constant fluctuations of death and rebirth, it seems necessary to posit a changeless inner essence.

However, when we look closely at the implications of these assertions, we may find that they create more problems than they solve. Are not a God who has yet to create the universe and a God who has already created the universe necessarily different? And is it not a case of the former changing into the latter, just as a childless woman changes in some way when she becomes a mother? A God that is changeless and a God that creates the universe therefore seem to be incompatible. An unchanging I is equally problematic: Without undergoing some change, how can a person overcome his imperfections and become enlightened?

Science and Buddhism

Many people have a worldview that is heavily influenced by scientific principles and techniques of investigation. In their practical applications, Buddhism and science may be strikingly different: Whereas science has been most successful in uncovering the workings of external phenomena such as matter, Buddhism's focus has always been on internal phenomena, primarily the mind. But there are many areas where the two systems do not disagree, differing only in emphasis rather than fundamentals.

For example, if we compare the theories of the origin of the universe presented by scientific and Buddhist traditions, a similar view emerges. Various explanations of how this world, the other planets, and the stars originated are put forth in different scientific theories. A common theme of these seems to be that though we can identify how various heavenly bodies began, the universe in general is not something for which scientists can pinpoint a particular beginning. Whatever phenomenon they trace events back to must itself also have had a cause.

We find the same broad conclusion at the atomic level. Many minute particles temporarily conglomerate to form a material object that disintegrates through the passage of time. Individual gross forms arise and fall apart or are destroyed, but it is not possible to posit a beginning to the process. Any atomic substance or element has to have causes. These causes must also have causes, and so on.

Buddhist scholars have no quarrel with this, but they take it one step further by also applying this understanding to the mind. Just as scientists say that the physical matter-energy continuum has been around in one manifestation or another as long as time has existed, so, Buddhists say, has the mind.

The scientific description of the conception and development of a child in the womb deals principally with the manifest physical aspects, from the meeting of the sperm and ovum onward. The Buddhist account, while not faulting this explanation, brings three other elements to the fore: consciousness, subtle form, and karma. A consciousness that has separated from its former body and that contains the karmic seeds deposited on it by previous actions, together with its support, a very subtle kind of form, enters the womb at the time of conception and joins with the uniting sperm and ovum. As the child grows in the womb, science can furnish a very accurate picture of the different stages of its physical development. The Buddhist texts speak more about the inner experience of the child at this time. Again, from the Buddhist point of view, these two versions of the first stage of life are compatible. There is nothing in the Buddhist description that contradicts the scientific one. On the contrary, the Buddhist finds the scientific description complementary to his own.

How far science has gone on to engage with the enigma of no intrinsic existence whatsoever is, of course, another matter. For the Consequentialists, the assumption that there is an observer-independent world of objective truth is fundamentally wrong, and they challenge this view head on. Many scientists today incline in the same direction; others accept the possibility of pure objective truth.

The greatest difference between Buddhism and majority scientific opinion concerns the mind. Science has indeed enjoyed great success in understanding and manipulating matter. On the basis of that success, scientific materialists try to explain everything in terms of the interactions of matter or physical energy. Many view the mind as an emergent property of the brain, even though the mind displays irreducibly different properties from its physiological correlates.

Idealists argue the opposite; they try to assimilate matter to mind. They believe that mind is primary: it is what we look out on the world with. The external-seeming world of material forms is explained away as a mere appearance to consciousness, something like a stable and convincing dream.

Consequentialists steer a way between these two extremes. Mind and matter, or mental and physical energy, are both at work in the universe, interdependent and interacting with each other. Mind is the subject, and matter, mind, and anything else we can conceive of is the object the subject engages with. Knower and known, observer and observed: we will not find one without the other. Neither is more fundamental than the other, neither one a byproduct of the other.

Nature of Mind

According to Buddhist philosophy, the defining characteristics of mind are that it is clear and knowing—it is clear with respect to what appears to it, and it acts to be aware of, to experience its objects. To be sure, Buddhist thinkers see physical brain activity as a necessary support for consciousness in the human realm. But if someone asks exactly what transforms into the present moment of an individual's mind—what is it that, in transforming, becomes this present moment of mind—we answer that it is only the previous moment of that mind. The quality of knowing objects, being aware of them, is exclusive to consciousness, so we would say of a computer, no matter how complex, that it can play chess, but it does not know how to play chess.

In the general Buddhist view then, mind is a nonmaterial phenomenon. Like matter, it is ever adapting and ever evolving, but it is not made of atoms and does not arise primarily out of their interactions. The main cause of any moment of mind is only the previous moment of that mind. Thus each individual's mind exists before and beyond the boundaries of this life. Indeed, mind is beginningless and endless. Change is a constant aspect of consciousness, as it is of the universe at large.

Sometimes a stream of consciousness deals with manifest, obvious objects, as when the ordinary sense consciousnesses take on the aspect of colors, shapes, smells, and tastes. Sometimes it takes a much subtler form, as during the death process. Sometimes the afflictions flare up. At other times they are not manifest and exist only as potentials. The influence of ignorance is always present to some degree in an ordinary person's consciousness, coloring every cognition a person has.

Associated with every consciousness and acting as its support is a very subtle kind of form or physical energy. Like the mind it ever accompanies, it cannot be said to have any beginning. Nor can we who possess our particular stream of consciousness be said in that sense to have any beginning. A person goes from life to life adopting or discarding different outward forms and personalities like roles in a stage show.

Science's understanding of life's physical processes has led to remedies to cure or ameliorate many severe diseases. Buddhism's doctrine of the continuity of mind over lifetimes, together with the theory of karma, has furnished an explanation of why misfortunes such as acute diseases fall on whom they do. There are Dharma practices that purify our negative inner karmic potentials before they ripen as such misfortunes, but the main aim is to bring to an end the process of uncontrolled rebirth and thereby abandon suffering completely. The means to take control of the situation lies in our capacity for mental transformation and evolution. The rapid technological advances of the last couple of centuries have opened our eyes to the sheer transformability of matter. The mind's parallel capacity for radical development should not be overlooked.

The mind is an eminently impressionable, responsive, and trainable entity. And as we know, once we are really familiar with something— be it a particular set of memorized verses, a mood, or a skill—the mind can operate almost without any effort at all. What is hard in the beginning can become spontaneous. The mind has an unlimited capacity to transform. Defilements and heavy, burdensome emotions like jealousy, self-pity, and anger can be eliminated, and wonder-working qualities like compassion can, with strong application, be enhanced to an infinite degree—over a series of lifetimes if necessary.

There are physical limitations to how high even the most athletic of us can jump, or how fast we can run. But the mind is not a physical phenomenon; it is not bound by those limitations. However deep the karmic imprints from our past negative involvements, however ingrained the mental afflictions of lifetimes in samsara, and however constrained our sense faculties in the present life, none of these limitations are intrinsic to the mind. Buddha stressed again and again the potential purity of the mind, a purity that is finally and fully revealed in buddhahood. All Dharma practices are, in a sense, simply a way to accumulate the causes and conditions necessary to make manifest that sublime potential.

One of the major classifications of mind in the Buddhist system is the division into valid and invalid awarenesses: those that correctly apprehend a particular aspect of reality and induce certainty with respect to it, and those that do not. A careful study of these two types of mind is most worthwhile. There are two distinct kinds of valid minds, direct valid minds and inferential valid minds. Some of the key objects of contemplation and meditation on the path to liberation, such as emptiness and impermanence, are quite subtle affairs, so an ordinary being cannot at first expect to observe them by direct perception, though that is his eventual aim. In the beginning, we have to depend on inference. Suppose we are standing outside a house and see smoke rising from the chimney. Seeing smoke, we infer that there is a fire inside the house. We do not see the fire directly, but we have accurate knowledge of it nonetheless. The first kind of wisdom we cultivate to guide us on the path to liberation will be of this type, the type that depends on reasons. This is just one way that Buddhism uses the study of the mind as a basis for the spiritual path.

Buddhist mind science also distinguishes thoroughly between the bare perception of the sense consciousnesses and the discursive activity of conceptual consciousness, and then there are the inspiring stages of single-pointed concentration and meditation that a practitioner ascends through on more exalted levels of the training. There are many more examples that illustrate the exactness, thoroughness, and helpfulness of Buddhist treatises on psychology and epistemology. Suffice it to say that, just as Western science has evolved its own methodologies of investigation of the external world, so too has Buddhism developed techniques of analysis and reasoning to comprehend the laws by which the mind operates, providing the basis for our evolution to the highest state of happiness. Surely positive and peaceful transformation will come about through these inner and outer sciences working in combination.

Buddhist Views of Cause and Effect

In the couplet that heads this chapter, Tsongkhapa sets out the analysis of causality that is exclusive to the Consequence school, that to be reliant on causes entails emptiness of inherent being. Other Buddhist schools adopt the opposite stance, that to arise in dependence on causes actually entails inherent existence.

By "other schools" we mean the schools that formed in India in classical times, prior to the transmission of Buddhism from India to Tibet. Conveniently for beginners, the Tibetan tradition has classified the abundance of views recorded in the classical Indian Buddhist texts into four main groups, the last of which has two subdivisions. They are as follows:

English	Sanskrit (Tibetan)
Great Exposition school	Vaibhashika (*byed brag smra ba*)
Sutra school	Sautrantika (*mdo sde pa*)
Mind Only school	Chittamatra (*sems tsam pa*)
Middle Way school	Madhyamaka (*dbu ma pa*)
Autonomy school	Svatantrika (*rang gyud pa*)
Consequence school	Prasangika (*thal 'gyur pa*)

Tsongkhapa, as one of the foremost exponents of the Consequence school's view in the Land of Snows, sometimes refers to all the remaining schools as the lower schools. We shall follow his nomenclature, though the views of these schools are often legitimately based on teachings Buddha gave. They have a value for particular individuals or particular circumstances, just as other religious beliefs and paths do. Therefore it is not merely a case of dismissing other explanations as inferior and unworthy.

The lower schools do not at all accept that things exist exactly in the way they appear to the ordinary mind. However, they do not view the appearance of things as inherently existent as a distortion. All phenomena are indeed selfless, they say, but that does not mean they have no existence from their own side whatsoever. When all is said and done, we can see with our own eyes that things are inherently existent. If we refuse to accept our bare sense perceptions as generally valid, how can we possibly discriminate between what exists and what does not? We can identify the circumstances where our sense perceptions are in error. For instance, a spoon half in and half out of a bowl of water looks bent. A drunken man may see two moons in the sky. But we can separate out these mistaken appearances and know the rest as valid. Our sense perceptions are by and large in direct contact with reality. Certainly things are created from causes and conditions, but how could they properly be said to exist if they did not have objective identities of their own, independent of mind?

Nagarjuna, the great commentator from the Andhra region of South India who pioneered the Middle Way school of interpretation and helped bring the Great Vehicle or Mahayana teachings into the mainstream of Buddhist practice, sets forth the two opposing views with his customary succinctness in his *Treatise on the Middle Way*, composed in the second century C.E. Not all of the lower schools listed above had come into existence when he was writing. However, they all fall into the same error as those Nagarjuna took as his actual opponents: they all cling to inherent existence. Tsongkhapa found that even some renowned later masters of the Middle Way school were not free of this error. Only the Consequence branch of that school can explain emptiness and dependent arising correctly.

The opponent:

All of these, if they were void,
would not arise or pass away.
For you it follows there would be
no four truths of the noble ones. (24:1)

The Consequence school responds:

> If they were *not* void, all of these
> would not arise or pass away.
> For *you* it follows there would be
> no four truths of the noble ones! (24:20)

So, from the lower schools' point of view, it is valid to argue that a house inherently exists because it arises in dependence on causes and conditions. The bricks and building materials that it is made of inherently exist and so do the atoms that make up those materials. If the parts were not inherently existent, they might argue, when you put them together, how would you have a house? We may dream about building a house. We may dream that we have the various building materials. However, we obviously cannot build a real house with dream bricks. Why not? Because, as we discover when we wake, they were just in the nature of appearances, not established as building materials from their own side.

Compare the image of an actor projected onto a film screen with the actor himself. When we see these two different appearances, how can the Consequentialists validly identify which is actually a person and which is not? For the lower schools it is easy. The projected image is not a person but is the mere appearance of a person, because, from the side of the object, there is no person to be found to validate the appearance. On the other hand, the real person is established from his own side because when we investigate, we find the person himself backing up the image of him that is before our mind. He is objectively established by way of his own very nature. The Consequentialists, in asserting that nothing exists from its own side, have no way to discriminate between the film image of a person and an actual person. Both are mere projections! To pass beyond suffering we must meditate deeply on selflessness but this claim that nothing has any objective existence whatsoever is far too radical.

Moreover, according to the lower schools, if the four truths were not established from their own side but were just some kind of mental designations, how could we speak of attaining this truth and abandoning that truth, and what benefit would there be in it? If we were merely imputed in the radical way the Consequentialists describe, how could we wander from one life to the next? How could we experience pleasure and pain? If positive and negative actions were devoid of their own inherent existence, then they would just be products of our imagination, merely there because we suppose them to be there, so what meaning could there be in engaging in one and abandoning the other? According to this critique then, those who propound no inherent existence are so deeply sunk in error that, in their system, the path to liberation is lost to sight, and even the distinctions between right and wrong and existence and nonexistence lose all meaning.

Tsongkhapa's verses show him filled with wonder at the discovery that, just as Nagarjuna argues, the exact opposite is the case: nothing makes sense without emptiness of inherent existence. The rest of this book is essentially Tsongkhapa's condensed articulation of Nagarjuna's critique of the opponents' view. A further variety of different Buddhist schools of interpretation grew up in India and then Tibet between Nagarjuna's day and Tsongkhapa's. Like Nagarjuna, Tsongkhapa in his verses does not explore differences between the views of the other schools; he dwells on their common shortcoming, their inability to integrate dependent arising and emptiness.

We should be aware that, unlike Nagarjuna's synthetic opponent, many of the non-Consequentialist philosophers whose presentations Tsongkhapa is responding to did not explicitly defend inherent establishment and attack the opposite thesis in their treatises. Sometimes their clinging to this subtlest level of reification was an unrecognized implication of some other argument they set forth, rather than a conscious prejudice in its favor.

It is also important to note that the Consequentialists say that for beginners who do not have a very profound understanding of the teachings, the lower schools' explanation of dependent arising may well be a suitable basis for engaging with the Dharma. Hearing the Buddha's teaching that they can reach liberation by practicing virtue and abandoning nonvirtue can cause joy in some people and inspire them to take a new and wholesome direction in life. They feel great pleasure, as if remembering something wonderful that they had always known but had somehow temporarily forgotten or overlooked. If such people hear the Consequentialist teaching of no inherent existence prematurely, it may sound to them like nihilism. Out of fear or confusion, they could end up abandoning the path of virtue altogether. On the other hand, finding nothing in the lower schools' exposition that contradicts their instinctive assumption that all things inherently exist, such newcomers to Buddha's teaching feel all the more comfortable in their new outlook on life, and they thereby generate pleasure and enthusiasm in their practice.

Buddha well understood that his ultimate teaching of no inherent existence would be beyond the range of some of his listeners' thought in the beginning. He taught the systems presented in the lower schools as easier steps where disciples might rest content for a time, or as rungs by which they might ascend to the subtlety of the ultimate essence of wisdom. However, in the final analysis, in order to cut off our compulsive wandering in cyclic existence, we must cultivate the most refined wisdom—the realization of the emptiness of inherent existence. No lesser insight will suffice.

Being a subtle phenomenon, emptiness is not easy to understand. We tend to have much more faith in the gross objects grasped by our senses. At a deep level of mind and over countless lifetimes we have become very familiar with the opposite, erroneous view, and we cling tenaciously to what we are familiar with. But by contemplating the reasons employed by the Consequentialists, we will begin to doubt our habitual misperceptions. Through perseverance we will undermine our trust in an objectively established world and know it to be a fabrication. Then the process of wiping away the layers of ignorance that encrust the natural purity of our mind can proceed. It may at first seem bizarre and outlandish to suppose that things are empty of any inherent being. In the end, however, we may well celebrate with Tsongkhapa:

5cd What way of fine instruction more
    astounding that this utterance?

4. Dependent Relativity and Selflessness

THE MIND of crystal clarity that sees ultimate reality directly is initially developed by thinking long and hard about why reality has to be the way it is. How dependent relativity is the chief reasoning that establishes ultimate truth is the subject of this book.

This is not to say, however, that the Buddhist path to freedom consists solely of training in reasoning and logic. The complete path has three divisions, known as the *three higher trainings*: the trainings in ethics, concentration, and wisdom. And the type of Buddhism that flourished in Tibet, Mahayana Buddhism, emphasizes the practice of compassion and concern for others to an extraordinary degree. We should strive to possess the compassionate motivation to benefit all sentient beings. If we can follow suitable moral guidelines and restrain from harming others, our minds will become steadier and less scattered. This gives us a sound basis for building up strong concentration, which when coupled with our wisdom understanding will lead to insights. The teachings on ethical discipline, concentration, and compassion are not the main subjects of this book, but it is important to keep in mind that they are all essential components of the path to enlightenment.

The subject of this book falls into the category of wisdom, which is, not surprisingly, where reasoning and logic are most needed. Before we can meditate productively on the ultimate nature of reality, we must first form a clear picture of what ultimate truth is. For most of us, this will require plenty of study, discussion, and reflection, and a willingness to try to reason things out. To proceed by intuition or meditation alone will only lead to frustration.

Suppose we have to tell a child to go to Moscow to meet his father.

Just saying that Moscow is in Russia, giving him a reason for going, and telling him to go will not achieve a great deal. He's a young child; he doesn't have the slightest idea of where Moscow and Russia are, and still less does he know how to get there, what documents he requires, and so forth. If he did set off on his own without any instructions, he would quickly get lost or become discouraged and give up, much as he might actually want to go. Or what if someone were given a gun and told to go shoot a deer, but he had no idea what a deer looked like or where to find one? He might go out and fire his gun at something else. He might even shoot another person! So what about someone who, hearing that people reach nirvana by meditating on the emptiness of self and all phenomena, immediately sits down with eyes closed? Even if she has inspiration and enthusiasm, is not her quest equally certain to end in discouragement and failure? The city of Moscow and a deer are much easier to recognize than the subtler levels of ignorance that afflict our minds. We need to investigate far more deeply to locate and eradicate this type of ignorance.

Generosity, patience, restraint from harming others, compassion: these are practices to be treasured. Anyone who wants to imitate Buddha or other great spiritual teachers must strive for these qualities. But the Indian Consequentialist master Chandrakirti calls these good qualities "sightless." One needs the guidance of wisdom and correct insight into emptiness to progress toward buddhahood. He says in his *Supplement to the "Treatise on the Middle Way"*:

> As when a group of blind folk all are led
> with ease by one with sight to where they wish,
> here wisdom takes the sightless qualities
> and likewise goes to the Subduer's stage. (6:2)

Developing the wisdom that realizes the ultimate is not a hypothetical, abstract philosophy. It is a process of looking within to transform our experience, our precious human intelligence guided by a path of reasoning as practically helpful as it is far-reaching. We are unlikely to understand just by reading someone's advice. We have to find the mental space in which to do some reflection. Is there really a way for the mind to become immaculately pure, free of all limitation, all obscuration? Do all negative emotions that shut down the mind's natural creativity arise from an initial, distorted misapprehension of the self? What could that misunderstanding be?

Other Buddhist Schools

Reasoning uncovers a difference between the way things appear and the way they actually exist. Things appear to have their own inherently established identity, but the fact of dependent relativity indicates otherwise. Even the simplest level of dependent relativity that all Buddhist schools accept, the dependence of things upon the causes that produce them, would be enough to establish that things are not inherently existent, if only we could see clearly. A sprout comes forth from a seed. For a seed to germinate, an array of contributory factors has to come together. Soil is required in which there is the correct degree of moisture and warmth. If there is too much water, the seed will rot; too little, and it will remain a seed. Its germination clearly relies on a host of things other than itself. But when we see a sprout, due to our innate ignorance it appears to exist from its own side. Though it is not self-produced, it appears to possess a nature that exists from within itself.

Like most people, followers of all the Buddhist schools other than the Consequence school assent to this appearance of inherent existence. They say that the great Subduer's astounding instruction on dependent relativity was not meant to refute such a fundamental mode of being. So then Tsongkhapa castigates them for "grasping at," i.e., misconceiving, dependent arising. Their limited insight is insufficient.

> 6 Fools' grasping at it fastens tight
> their fetters of extremism.
> The same for wise ones is the means
> to sever fabrication's net.

These bamboozled ones "fasten tight" their bonds to samsara by misunderstanding what should be their very means to freedom.

The Consequentialists, we may recall, are a subgroup of the Middle Way school. The middle way they follow leads between two extremes. One is the abyss of nihilism. Those who veer to this extreme refute so much that they are unable to posit any valid foundation for the existence of things. They thereby undercut the simple rules of morality and logic and make it impossible to establish anything. The other extreme is the abyss of eternalism or reification. Those who veer in this direction are those who do not refute enough. With some understanding of dependent arising, they may refute simpler levels of self-grasping, but they leave the subtlest level unchallenged. They cannot let go of the ultimate cause of their frustration, their deepest level of self-grasping. Verse 6 indicates this is the extreme many Buddhist schools are stuck in.

The "wise ones," on the other hand, employ the reasoning of dependent relativity to slip the chains of these miserable alternatives and escape to freedom and clarity. The net of fabrications they sever includes mistaken appearances to our minds of inherent existence, the conceptions grasping at things as existing that way, and all the endless conceptions that flow from that confusion. One who cuts all these asunder reaches full enlightenment.

However, the fundamental qualm of the non-Consequentialist Buddhist schools is one that many of us will initially share. They ask, "If objects did not have some identity independent of our observation of them, then how could they act as a valid, reliable basis for our apprehension of them?" Selflessness is a basic tenet of Buddhism, so all Buddhist schools propound a view of selflessness, some of considerable subtlety. We cannot cover all of the various views of what it means to be empty and selfless in a short commentary. But we will glance at two of the simpler views of selflessness because that will help us graduate toward the more profound view that Tsongkhapa extols. By examining the alternatives to the correct view and discovering their shortcomings, we will see the need for a more radical view, however much it may go against the grain of our presuppositions.

The first view of selflessness we will look at is one that discerns the nonexistence of a permanent, unitary, independent (literally, "own-powered") I, distinct from the flow of the five aggregates, our body and mind. The second focuses on the absence of a self-sufficient, substantially existent I anywhere within our continuum of body and mind. Tsongkhapa insists that we must continue to analyze until we realize a third, still more subtle level of selflessness, the I's lack of inherent existence. Each of these three levels of insight into selflessness overcomes its opposing misconception. We proceed by refuting the false self that the particular misconception grasps at. The first step is to bring the false self clearly into view. This is called *identifying the object of refutation*. The three objects of refutation, going from coarse to subtle, are thus as follows:

1. The permanent, unitary, independent self
2. The self-sufficient, substantially existent self
3. The inherently existent self

Permanent, Unitary, and Independent

The first wrong view, the misconception that the self is *permanent, unitary*, and *independent*, is notable because major non-Buddhist, Indian philosophical schools assert a self of this kind. The Buddhist thinkers of old, when Buddhism was a growing and flourishing religion in India, naturally defined themselves in contrast to these other schools. They adhere to a self (*atman*); Buddhism asserts no-self (*anatman*). In Tibet, the followers of the Indian schools whose views did not become established north of the Himalayan divide became known as "outsiders," while disciples of the Buddha become known as "insiders" or "inner beings."

The outsiders are referred to in the next verse as "forders" (*tirthika*), another term used by Buddhists to refer to those Indian pandits who hold non-Buddhist views.

7   No others with this teaching seen,
    so you alone we Teacher name.
    False praise to call a forder that
    or give a fox the name of lion.

Adherents of other creeds posit their own "fords" by which to cross to the far shore of felicity. There is no one among them who correctly teaches dependent arising, and thus no one who deserves the title of "Teacher," just as none but the king of beasts is worthy of the name "lion." To call a fox such would be mere flattery.

The self that most non-Buddhist Indian schools assert is first of all *unitary*. Unitary means partless; it cannot be broken into smaller components. It is *independent*, meaning not under the power of, or depending upon, the aggregates. It is *permanent*. Permanent in a Buddhist context means changeless, static, and without production and disintegration. It is the opposite of impermanent, but it does not necessarily signify existing forever. The disagreement between Buddhists and the Indian schools that posit a permanent self is not about whether the self goes on from life to life; both agree that it does. The question is whether what goes on is changing from moment to moment. Buddhists say it is; the non-Buddhists say it is not.

Some see a permanent self as necessary to guarantee continuity from life to life and moment to moment. Such a self is the bearer of a person's true identity through time. A tree loses its leaves in the autumn, shows bare branches in the winter, and puts forth fresh greenery in the spring, but something recognizable persists: the tree.

Buddhists agree that the tree endures, but only by changing as it goes. Is there anything still there in the second moment that was there in the first? Of course—the tree. But is the tree in the second moment the same as the tree in the first moment? Indeed it is not. The hardest rock or gemstone may maintain a similar appearance for a million years, but it is still disintegrating moment by transient moment. No matter how dense the granite or how rigidly structured the diamond, every instant it passes away into a new transformation, just like a flickering candle flame or foam on a wave. Even at the subatomic level, there is no fundamental particle or packet of energy that is not subject to this process of decay. If the necessary causes and conditions assemble, then a second moment similar in type to the first arises, and we observe continuity. If a radically different set of causes and conditions obtains, we observe disintegration without reintegration. What place is there for a permanent, unaffected whole or self in all this?

A unitary or partless self could not be made up of the aggregates. It would have to be an entity quite distinct from them. Simply speaking, a person's aggregates are his body and mind, but they are traditionally enumerated as five: form, feeling, discrimination, compositional factors, and mind. *Form* is our material aspect—our physical body. *Feeling* and *discrimination* are classified as separate aggregates because of their critical role in how we engage with the world. So much depends on how we identify objects in the first place and then how we respond to them, with feelings of pleasure, displeasure, or indifference. *Compositional factors* are everything left that does not fit into the other four aggregates, the varied factors that contribute to our overall mental states, such as faith, pride, hope, doubt, anger, and equanimity, and also the factors within us that are neither form nor consciousness, such as the impermanence of the aggregates or the residual karmic seeds accumulated in the mind. The last aggregate, *mind*, incorporates the basic mental and sense consciousnesses. Each of the five is called an *aggregate* to remind us that it, too, is only a transitory collection of parts.

The permanent, unitary, independent self, if it existed, would have to be distinct from the aggregates, just temporarily associating with them. For simplicity we may liken it to a dry pea in a jar. When the jar of the aggregates is smashed, the pea of the self goes on alone to the next life. But if the self really were like that, then we ought to be able to put the aggregates aside one by one and still isolate the self right there as another item separate from them. But such a thing is not found. If we remove the parts of a bicycle one by one until we've taken all of them away, no bicycle remains. The self is like that.

When Jane's leg is in pain, Jane herself is in pain. But if Jane's self and her leg were somehow different entities made up of separate substances, why should Jane be in pain when her leg is? Susan does not feel pain when Jane's leg is injured, because she and Jane's leg are separate entities. So why should this partless Jane, who is also an entity separate from her leg, feel pain? When Jane's funny face makes someone laugh, it is Jane who makes them laugh, not Susan, because Jane's funny face is within the entity Jane, part of her and not part of Susan. Jane's leg and her funny face do not just belong to her, they are *within* her. A unitary self that exists in addition to and distinct from the parts does not square with this fact.

We are led along by our parts at all times. We are content when our stomach is full and downcast when our memory recalls pleasures we will never enjoy again. As soon as our body can no longer sustain us, we die. When the mind, ever transforming from moment to moment, finally abandons the old body, passes through the trauma of forgetting, and migrates to a new life, the momentarily changing self does the same. How can we conceive of the self as independent in the sense of being "own-powered" when what becomes of it depends so heavily upon the aggregates? We grow up, we grow old, we grow sick, we grow wise. We are swept along by karmic consequences like a stick in a rushing stream.

The self that each of us is is impermanent, made up of parts, and not independent. This is the self that evolves to liberation. An ultimate, pure, unchanging essence that is me, yet that is not constituted of the parts and is outside their sway, is simply not seen by any valid mind.

An ordinary person does not naturally misconceive of the self to exist in quite the way described above. The masters of Tsongkhapa's tradition insist that none of the innate, naturally arising modes of false self-grasping apprehend a self that is separable from the aggregates. The above type of reified self is the product of philosophical ingenuity rather than something projected by an untutored, instinctive kind of ignorance.

Self-Sufficient and Substantially Existent

The second kind of self-grasping we are going to describe here does have an instinctive, or innate, manifestation. The innate grasping at a *self-sufficient, substantially existent self* is a naturally arising trouble-maker that will interfere with our peace of mind. We don't have to contrive this false self through speculation. In that respect, it is the same as the inherently existent self that is the unique object of refutation of the Consequence school. We may or may not assent to these two misconceived views of self on an intellectual level, but as ordinary beings at our present level of evolution, our minds enter the world already imbued with these delusions. They color our consciousness, affecting the very way things appear to us, and they are ever ready to transform from a latent, dormant level into a manifest state. When that happens, we assent to the false appearance; we actively grasp at the self as if it actually existed in the way that it appears.

The Consequentialists regard both the permanent, unitary, independent self and the self-sufficient, substantially established self as false projections to be refuted. So if we can next expose the self-sufficient, substantially existent self for the hollow mockery that it is, we will relieve our mind of a menace, a chief instigator of our self-importance and self-pity.

Is it *the* chief instigator? According to the lower schools, yes. They all agree that the subtle, instinctive level of grasping at the self-sufficient, substantially existent self we are about to describe is the root cause of why we are caught up in the round of uncontrolled, painful existence. If we eradicate this grasping completely, then all the other afflictive obstructions will be removed. In a mind where there is no moisture of afflictions, the karmic seed that would otherwise ripen up at the point of death and fling us into another life is unable to germinate. They say that meditation on the nonexistence of a self-sufficient, substantially existent self can do this for us, though more may be required to lift us to buddhahood. Tsongkhapa counters that this is not so. We must go on to repudiate a still subtler mode of self-grasping by developing our understanding of dependent arising to a clearer, more complete level.

Something *substantially existent* can be independently identified, without depending on the identification of some other phenomenon. A person is an imputed existent; he cannot be identified without first identifying some other phenomenon, such as one of, or the collection of, the aggregates. Most Buddhist schools accept in their own way that the defining characteristic of a person is that he is a being imputed in dependence on any of his five aggregates. The term *person* here includes all beings from a buddha superior down to a bedbug's egg and smaller. Indeed, it includes the whole range of sentient creatures.

What do we mean by *imputed* in this context? Imagine we are standing by a harbor and see a large warship steaming into port. Above the ship flutters a piece of cloth. In the top corner are rows of white stars on a square blue background; the rest is covered by horizontal red and white stripes. As soon as we see such a design, "U.S. flag" springs to mind. In dependence on one thing appearing to our mind, something additional appears, a meaning requiring to be formulated by the mind, which would not be there without the mind's contribution, but which we see out there on the external object. At that point we are imputing "U.S. flag" onto that pattern. A similar process occurs when we are driving and a red traffic light immediately makes us think "stop."

Substantial existent and *imputed existent* are opposites. For the lower schools, the color blue is an example of a substantial existent. No matter how much we chop it up, no matter what angle we come at it from, any part we see is still blue. A boy named Joe, an army, and winter are examples of imputed existents. Joe, the army, and winter are not given to mind directly. They are conveyed there through the appearance of something else, some kind of cue such as a part. In dependence on the appearance of that unique shape of face or sound of voice, "Joe" appears to mind. In dependence on the appearance of many soldiers and weapons of war, an "army" appears to mind. In dependence on the shortness of days and frosty weather, "winter" appears to mind.

However, to refute the self-sufficient, substantial existence of the self, we must do more than simply refute that it has the type of substantial existence just described. When we grasp at a self-sufficient, substantially existent self, we grasp at a self that appears not just to be apprehensible in its own right but to have its own autonomous power over the aggregates. It appears to be self-sufficient to the point of governing the aggregates without relying on them.

Proponents of the permanent, unitary, independent self conceive it to be definitely other than the aggregates. On the other hand, when we instinctively grasp at the self-sufficient, substantially existent self, it seems to exist in some way from within the aggregates. It is the discriminator, the feeler, the one who hears and sees, the one who walks and breathes after all. Sailors have described how a small sailing boat can loom as large as a galleon in the baffling visual conditions of a shifting sea fog. This false self looms above the aggregates in the same exaggerated fashion.

In the fog of instinctive grasping, the truth that the self exists merely in the nature of the aggregates and at the mercy of their fluctuations is obscured. Instead, the self-sufficient, substantially existent self appears, although based on the aggregates, to emerge with a force of its own, controlling but not controlled. Assenting to that self-image is just what gives rise to self-centeredness and compulsive craving or hostility. An oft-used image is that of the self as the owner or governor of the aggregates, who are his servants or slaves. Since the self-sufficient substantially existent self is such a troublesome fellow, perhaps we can picture him as the mob boss and the aggregates as his band of underlings. He is not separate from them because he is a gangster just like them, but he is their superior, and they do his bidding.

If the self existed in any way over and above the aggregates, we ought to be able to mentally isolate it right there. In fact, the relationship between self and aggregates is too close for the self to have any truly autonomous dimension. It is the relationship between whole and parts. The self is simply fashioned from the aggregates because they are its parts; it does not pass beyond them.

The self is no different from a book in this sense. When we remove the pages and the cover, the book is gone. Book, pages, and cover all share the same entity. The "book" depends entirely on its parts; it is different from them, but it is not a different *entity* from them. There is not a single atom that is contained in a book but that is not contained in its parts. This does not make the book and its parts exactly the same, but it does make them the same entity. The self is likewise simply the whole constituted by its parts, the mental and physical aggregates. They compose it. It is made up of them. When my fingers move my chess piece, *I* move it. When my mind wants to win the game, then *I* want to win it, not otherwise. No actual I ever acts, thinks, or responds without the participation of the aggregates. A person may indeed direct his parts to perform various actions—something a book could never do—but in no sense is he a self-sufficient or autonomous controller of them. Rather, isn't it more like when a group of friends plan a camping trip? It is legitimate to say that the group has decided to go on a trip, but in no sense does "the group" have any *autonomous* decision-making power, distinct from its members.

This is the kind of analysis that refutes the self-sufficient, substantially existent self we instinctively grasp at. Having negated the false self with reasoning, we must then meditate intensively on the sheer absence of it. Eradicating an instinctive wrong view takes strong concentration over time. Then we arrive at a powerful vision of ourselves as nothing without the aggregates, subject to their momentary transformation under the influence of external stimuli and internal fluctuations: now tired, now fresh; now hungry, now sated; now this karma ripening as an unexpected pleasure, now that one as woe.

The self's stable well-being depends entirely on the stable well-being of the aggregates, but the mind and body are anything but stable. How did we come to have such aggregates in the first place? It happened through the power of the mental afflictions and contaminated karma— karma that, even if virtuous, spins the thread of cyclic existence rather than snapping it. The aggregates are a prime example of true suffering, the first of the four truths. Thus the teachings of the other Buddhist schools on selflessness lead directly to the path of Dharma. They lay bare a deep cause of our entanglement in the world's superficial allurements, which are, as Tsongkhapa has said elsewhere, not satisfying but addictive, not trustworthy but the gateway to suffering.

Perspectives on the Lower Schools' Views

Though the thinkers of the lower schools contemplate various levels of dependent relativity to reach their insights, this does not prompt in them the suspicion that the self altogether lacks inherent existence. When they refute the permanent, unitary, independent self, they refute any self having a separate nature from the aggregates. When they refute the self-sufficient, substantially existent self, they refute a self from within the aggregates that has independent control over them. But when the Consequentialists penetrate to the third, subtlest, level of selflessness, they understand that not just persons but all phenomena, including the aggregates, have no "own-nature" whatsoever.

In complete contrast, the other schools say that form, feeling, discrimination, mind, and many of the items collected in the compositional factors aggregate are all substantially existent. In this way, they claim, a substantial foundation remains even if a person is only imputed. They can show how someone who is only an imputed existent can still be reliably identified, since he or she is supported by the sound bedrock of substantial aggregates. So for them the basis for the imputation of the person cannot itself be imputed.

Some noted scholars from these non-Consequentialist schools make another interesting move. They accept some form of subtle mental consciousness—different schools have different descriptions of it—as a substantially existing self. The subtle mental consciousness is the substratum of mind that persists from life to life even when coarser levels of consciousness shut down and the body is discarded at death. Bhavaviveka, one of the renowned commentators of the Middle Way Autonomy school, says in his *Blaze of Reasoning* (chapter 18):

> …we also actually impute the term *self* to the [mental] consciousness conventionally. Because the [mental] consciousness takes rebirth, it is said that it is the self.

In effect, Bhavaviveka is saying that only the ordinary self of everyday life is imputedly existent. There is among the aggregates, not of different character to them and not appearing as their controller, a subtle self, not manifest to ordinary experience, that guarantees that we are findable from our own side. So for the lower schools, the object imputed must somehow be established from the side of its basis of imputation.

Tsongkhapa maintains two perspectives on the lower schools. He chastises them for not getting right to the bottom of what dependent relativity is about. On the other hand, he acknowledges that the insights they do attain are valid and valuable, not off the point. Their attack is a direct broadside at the harms of cyclic existence and so not to be dismissed but rather built upon. One way of explaining the four epithets for Buddha in the next verse utilizes the latter perspective:

8 O wondrous teacher, refuge too!
    O wondrous speaker, guardian!

> I bow to you who taught so well
> dependent relativity.

In this verse, "teacher" refers to Buddha as the teacher of the lower schools' tenets, which do not deny inherent existence. "Refuge" is praise to Buddha for teaching the highest system of tenets, in which the inseparability of emptiness and dependent arising is revealed. "Speaker" refers to Buddha's teaching of the other schools' views in accordance with the needs of those of lesser capacity, and "guardian" is a description merited by the ultimate protection of the teaching on dependent arising and emptiness, suitable for students of great capacity. This verse, the eighth, is the homage of the main text, just as the first verse was the homage of the introduction.

In presenting the two lesser views of the selflessness described in this chapter, we have introduced some of the many modes of dependent arising of the self. If we internalize and meditate on these facts, the next time we come under stress or temptation, we will be a little less likely to become seized by a bossy, self-satisfied, autonomous sense of "me." Such a notion of the self is a false notion that obscures who we actually are. When we act on the basis of a misunderstanding, we are all too likely to act unskillfully and end up causing problems for ourselves and others.

When we assent to the appearance of ourselves as self-sufficient and substantially existent, it is easy for a modest sense of our own accomplishments to turn into pride. If we vainly display our knowledge, or if we proudly display our expensive possessions, people may find it harder to like us. But if we think more realistically about the many people who helped us to build up that knowledge, or if we compare ourselves with the many people who are far better off than us, our pride will decrease. Though our knowledge will not have decreased, and the value of our house or car will not have gone down, people will find us less obnoxious. As Buddha proposed, if we keep an authentic awareness of who we are—beings interwoven in dependent relationships with the impermanent aggregates, with helping causes, and with other people—we will be better aligned with reality, which in turn bestows peace of mind and creativity.

Let it be clear that in seeking an understanding of selflessness, we are not attempting to get rid of a sense of I altogether; it is these glorified, exaggerated notions of self that we must vanquish. Say we mistakenly think Peter has stolen our watch, but later we find the watch where we had in fact left it. Our delusion is dispelled because the object it grasped at, "Peter the thief," is refuted, and Peter remains, with the overlay of "thief" removed. It is like that. We are not supposed to end up finding that we do not exist at all or that we are somehow inexpressibly neither one thing nor the other. When we have cleared the wrong notions away, then the validly existing I will be seen for what it is, and our transformative potential for enlightenment will be clearly revealed.

5. Dependent Relativity and Emptiness

ALL PHENOMENA ARISE in dependence on other phenomena. The meaning of a phenomenon being dependently related or dependently arisen is that it exists only by virtue of, or in reliance upon, many phenomena other than itself. The simple test of whether y is related to or dependent on x is to ask, "If x did not occur, by the power of that would y also not occur?" Smoke is related to fire because without fire, there is no smoke. It is not accurate to say that where or when there is no fire, there is no smoke. What about inside a smoker's mouth? Rather we say that if there is no fire, there is no smoke. *Related* is sometimes taken to mean "meeting" or "coming together," so being dependently related then gives the sense of being established in dependence on the meeting or coming together of many phenomena.

The meaning of *arising* does not go beyond the meaning of being *established* here. Caused phenomena are readily understood to be effects that arise in dependence upon their causes. But all phenomena, even permanent ones—those that are not caused and are not changing moment to moment—come into being only in dependence on phenomena other than themselves, so they are also reckoned as dependent arisings, at least by followers of the Middle Way schools. Examples of permanent phenomena are abstract phenomena like instance and generality, not any particular instance or generality but instance and generality themselves. True cessations (the third of the four truths)—the absences of the afflictions and their seeds in the mindstreams of realized beings—are another example, as is uncompounded space, characterized as the absence of obstruction and contact.

Buddhist philosophers understand the word *condition* to mean something like "cause." For some, cause and condition have the same extension. For others, the main object that transforms into a particular thing is the cause of that result, while the other contributory factors, which may arise only just prior to the formation of the effect, are the conditions. For instance, in Tibetan medicine there are illnesses that are of a hot nature and those that are of a cold nature. When someone who has a complaint of the latter kind goes out in cold weather, the illness manifests and she starts to feel unwell. The illness has a causal sequence that begins long before the time of going outside. The cold weather is the immediate occasion or condition that causes the symptoms to manifest strongly so that she feels indisposed. However, it is important to note that the lines:

> 5ab "What on conditions does rely
> is empty of inherent being."

refer to all phenomena, whether caused or uncaused. Caused phenomena are created in dependence upon conditions. Permanent phenomena are not created from causes and conditions, but they still rely on conditions since they only arise when certain conditions are present and they cease to exist when those conditions are not fulfilled. They are said to be *established* in dependence on conditions though not *created* in dependence on them.

Varieties of Dependent Arising

We have made a preliminary exploration of how a phenomenon such as a person depends fundamentally on causes and conditions, and on parts. For a fuller appreciation of dependent arising, we will now explore some other versions of it, such as the interdependence of agent, action, and object; of generality and instance; of opposites; and of observer and observed.

For there to be a song, there has to be someone who sings it and the action of singing. None of these three can exist in isolation from the others. The action of singing and the object produced by that action, the song, arise as effects of the agent, the singer. The singer in turn is also established in dependence upon them, even though they are his effects. Someone is a mother because of the child she has produced. Here again the cause depends on the effect just as much as the effect depends on the cause. Thus agent, action, and object are all mutually dependent.

Someone says, "There is some fruit on the table if you are hungry." The kind is not specified, so what appears to mind on hearing the term fruit? Just the generality, "fruit." When we look on the table, we find fruit there wholly on the strength of its instances being there. Yet no individual instance or group of instances of fruit—banana, papaya, mango, and so on—can be equated with the generality "fruit," the one that pervades or extends over all the varieties; nor is "fruit" found separately as a distinct entity in addition to the individual varieties. So to explain the presence of the generality, we again must ponder the process of imputation, how fruit appears to mind in dependence on its instances. If the generality "fruit" is absent from the table, any instances—orange, apple, or melon—will be absent too, thus showing how a generality and its instances are mutually dependent.

In pairs of opposites such as hot and cold, beautiful and ugly, and fat and thin, each component of the pair needs the other to exist. In order to define *hot*, we have to distinguish it from cold. The category *cold* has to exist for hot to have any meaning. If there were no cold to contrast it with, how could hot be understood? No such phenomenon as hot or cold has an identity in its own right. Their identities only emerge through an awareness of the relationship between them.

Moreover, which of the two of a pair of opposites applies in a given case is often wholly subjective. We think *here* of the place we are and *there* for the other side of the room or valley. But for people over there, where they are is *here* and where we are is *there*. For one particular place, there are these two opposite apprehensions, one valid for each of two observers. Self and other are a similar case. For any one person in a room full of a hundred people, there will be one person thinking *self* and ninety-nine people, equally properly, thinking *other* of that person. These are two simple examples of how the nature of the object, the observed, is determined by the perspective of the observer. Is Tibetan butter tea tasty or unpleasant? It rather depends on the taster!

These examples prompt an appreciation of how any phenomenon arises solely as an interconnection in a network of relationships. Notice that these observations apply across the board, not just to persons but to all caused phenomena, and in many cases to all phenomena whatsoever. In the previous chapter, we refuted two false modes of existence of the self: the conception apprehending the self to be permanent, unitary, and independent, and the one apprehending the self to be self-sufficient and substantially established. The absence of either of these false modes of existence is known as a *selflessness*. Meditation on either of them is first and foremost a corrective to wrong views of the self or person. Thinking about the dependent relationships pointed out so far in this chapter will counteract a more pervasive false mode of existence that we impute not just to ourselves and other people but to all phenomena. The absence of this mode of existence, applying as it does to all phenomena and not to persons alone, is known either as a *selflessness* or as an *emptiness*.

Full Implications of Dependent Arising

We must now deploy the above examples of dependent relativity to lead ourselves into the more profound Consequentialist view of ultimate truth, which is the emptiness or voidness of inherent existence.

> 9 Our benefactor, voidness is
> the essence of the teachings that
> you gave for wandering beings' sake,
> dependent relativity

> 10 The peerless reason proving that.
> What way for those to grasp your view
> who see it either as unproved
> or contradictory? You said

> 11 Once voidness is perceived as what
> arising in dependence means,

then voidness of inherent being
and act and agent harmonize

12 Not contradict. If seen reversed,
the void not fit to act, and on
what acts no voidness, then you said
one plunges to a dread abyss.

We have striven to show how any phenomenon whatsoever is a dependently related arising, that the "peerless reason" of dependent relativity is "proved" upon, or established as a quality of, absolutely all phenomena. In order for this reasoning to sweep away the false notion of inherent existence, we must next become convinced that the fact that something is dependently related necessitates that it is not inherently existent, that being dependently related does indeed exclude any possibility of something existing by its own power.

The Indian non-Buddhist schools who posit an essentially permanent self might deny as "unproved" the assertion that the self is a dependent arising. For the non-Consequentialist Buddhist schools, the argument is "contradictory," since their position, in Tsongkhapa's analysis, is that being a dependent arising, simply being an existent in fact, entails inherent existence. Without the foundation of inherent existence, they suppose, no sensible presentation of phenomena is possible; there is only nihilism.

As seen in verse 11, the Consequence school, on the other hand, argues that not only is the functioning of things completely harmonious with their being empty of inherent being, but that such voidness is indeed essential to the performance of any act by any agent. "Voidness" is, after all, the very meaning of arising in dependence.

The hot nature of fire, with its power of burning, and the wet nature of water, with its power of moistening, appear to be inherently established, and seem to exist from the side of those objects themselves. Nevertheless, the argument of dependent relativity, when fully understood, compels the conclusion that fire and water's appearance of standing independently and having their own natures from within themselves is utterly deceptive. If fire possessed its hot and burning characteristics from its own side, it would not depend on any other phenomenon for those characteristics. This would mean that no fire could ever go out. If its hot and burning nature were independent of all other phenomena, then what could act to extinguish it? How could it ever die out for lack of fuel?

If a seed and a sprout both had their own intrinsically established natures, then the sprout would not arise in dependence on the seed, and the seed would not produce it. Neither one would need the other. Yet what meaning does the word *seed* have? A seed is merely a thing that has the capacity to transform into a sprout on the way to becoming a mature plant. But if the entities of seed and sprout each existed from their own side, by their own power, they would be unrelated, and a seed's nature could not pass away into the nature of a sprout. Since it could not be affected by any other factors, a seed would neither gain nor lose characteristics, and it would never transform into anything else or cease to exist.

In the case of impermanent phenomena, we have to recognize that there is no question of superficial change while the essence or core remains there unchanging. A change to a part is a change to the whole. Every atom, even in the hardest stainless steel, is in a constant state of flux and disintegration. Likewise there is no way for any phenomenon, cause or uncaused, to be dependent on other phenomena for some temporary qualities while still maintaining an inner, inherently established essence. It is not as if a rock's being wet or dry or hot or cold could depend on external factors while its rockness remained independent of them. If that were so, the rock, like the fire and the seed, would never pass out of existence, since nothing could ever impinge on it. But even huge mountain ranges are eroded flat and washed as mud to the sea by nothing more than the action of frost and rain.

The phenomena that an object depends on need not be external to it. As we have seen, when a stream of negative emotion such as annoyance or spite gathers power and threatens to carry us away, the sense of I necessary to precipitate that negative mood is of a self-powered entity, not reliant upon anything. But the I can in no way really be an independent entity, since it is altogether reliant upon the internal parts, mind and body, for its existence. I only feel warm in that my body feels warm. I only understand the answer in that my mind does.

Yet my mind is not the I. If it were, it would not make sense to say, "I kicked the football." My body is also not the I. If it were, it would not make sense to say, "I am thinking of my mother." Dependence on other factors, internal or external, is thus directly contradictory with inherent existence or existence from the object's own side. Nothing can be partly dependent and partly independent; recognizing that the I is dependent is the very way to cut off clinging to the false view of its independence or inherent being.

On the other hand, those who refuse to accept that something void of inherent existence can be dependently related are those who, in verse 12, see things "reversed." They see the "void not fit to act." The meaning of *void* here is not voidness or emptiness in the abstract, but those things that are void of inherent existence, such as a pot or a tree. Such people think that if a pot were without an intrinsic essence, it would simply be unreal and therefore unable to act, unable to do anything like holding water. Since such things do function, since pots do hold water, those people think they cannot possibly be void of inherent existence.

As verse 12 continues, they see "on what acts no voidness." For them, voidness of inherent existence cannot be established on anything that is capable of doing something. So those who see things "reversed" in this way deny that void things have the ability to function and superimpose on functioning things an inherent mode of being that they do not possess. Either way, they tumble into the abyss of confusion. In denying, they fall to the extreme of annihilation or nihilism. In superimposing, they fall to the extreme of eternalism or reification. Thus are they relegated to a "dread abyss" where they flounder, far from the Middle Way, far from the light of liberation, blind to dependent arising's rescuing power.

13   From what you taught, praise most you saw
     arising in dependence then,
     for that the nihilists can't see
     nor holders to inherent being.

14   The nonreliant are sky flowers,
     thus nondependence but a naught.

Establishment by essence blocks
reliance on condition or cause.

The "sky flowers" of verse 14 are a traditional Indian example of a nonexistent, like a hare's horn. Nonreliant phenomena, says Tsongkhapa, are no more findable than are flowers growing in midair. A proper assessment of emptiness and dependent relativity finds them inseparable, like two sides of the same coin, a positive mode of being—depending, relying—perfectly complemented by its negative mode—not inherent, not by its power.

This is what the extremists cannot see. Without this insight, their explanations are doomed to fail the test of reasoning. This is Tsongkhapa's special understanding and rediscovery of the Middle Way. Of course, it is not original to him; it comes from the Buddha. But among the plethora of competing interpretations of Buddha's deepest teachings, what more coherent, logically precise, and plainly sensible explanation could there be? This affirmation of the sublime harmony of dependent arising and emptiness, cogently and clearly set out at length in his subsequent prose works and meticulously sourced both from the sutras of Buddha and the classic Indian commentaries, is the kernel of Tsongkhapa's greatness as a philosopher.

15   You taught thus only objects that
dependently arise exist—
thereby no objects save those that
are empty of inherent being.

Seeking the I

The challenge still remains for us to penetrate to a proper ascertainment of emptiness. "Peerless" though dependent relativity may be as a reason in the proof of the absence of inherent existence, most of us will need to consider the question again and again from many different angles in order to build up a firm conviction that things are indeed empty of inherent being. We need to inquire persistently into the nature of the object. Any object will do. Since distorted grasping at the self is the root of the afflictive emotions, it makes sense to concentrate on the I. Other objects that stir up undue attachment or aversion are useful to work on, but any ordinary, matter-of-fact object is also completely suitable.

The reasoning of dependent arising precludes any existence from the side of the object whatsoever. This is too radical for the other Buddhist schools to accept. When the Consequentialists explain that all phenomena are merely imputed by conception, "merely" in that phrase specifically eliminates any shadow of objective existence, or existence by way of a thing's own essence. Since all phenomena are empty of that type of existence, the only way any phenomenon can exist is by being merely posited there through the power of a subjective awareness. As we have remarked, the other Buddhist schools have their own understanding of how some phenomena at least are imputed, but still, in their perspective, there has to be something, somewhere within the basis in dependence on which such a phenomenon is imputed that, in the end, *is* that imputed phenomenon.

If we deny that everything is merely imputed from the mind's side, then we ought to be able to look over on the object's side and find something, either within or in addition to the parts, that we can identify as that object. If it really is there by way of its own inherent nature, we should be able to pinpoint the inherently existent object. In the case of the I, for instance, we may begin by looking for an I that is separate from the aggregates. But as we have already noted, the valid self is composed of the aggregates. We will not find any self beyond or separate from the aggregates. Therefore we can dismiss as an artificial projection the autonomous I that operates independently of the aggregates. At death, the self does indeed separate from the gross physical form and leave it behind, but it remains associated with the mental aggregates and goes along with them to the next life.

If we look at the aggregates, is there anything among them that is the objective self? As we have noted, some Buddhist thinkers have allowed that the I be identified with some form of an ever-becoming subtle level of mind, a level that persists even in deep sleep and arises every moment, even through the trauma of death. This excludes consciousnesses that are occasional, that come and go throughout the day, or arise contingently.

In the case of a self that is identified merely as a subtle, persisting level of consciousness, what about the physical aspect? When a person bends double under a heavy load, is her subtle level of consciousness bending double? When she waves goodbye, does her subtle consciousness also wave? Remember that consciousness has no color or shape, so nobody can see it! This is a case of positing something as the self that is unable to fulfill the requisite criteria. The consciousness instigates the act of waving, but of course it is the arm that performs the physical act. If I am fatter than you, does that mean my subtle mental consciousness is fatter than yours? The self put forward here can only have mental qualities, but a self of the type we are is fully engaged in the physical world too. Also, on the one hand, I am a mind, and on the other, I possess a mind? Only confusion results if a part is made to do duty for the whole.

Another superficially tempting candidate for the objectively existing self is the bare aggregates. When we see that a person is only imputed, just a designation to a group of parts collected together, we may see the unitary I merely as a kind of fiction conveniently projected by the mind. But Jane cannot be validly projected just anywhere. Only when we project Jane on the basis of Jane's aggregates do we have a valid cognition of her. So it is the bare aggregates that are Jane as she exists from her own side then. It seems incomplete to say that just one aggregate, such as the mental consciousness, is her, but what about the five of them? When Jane takes the bus or checks her email, is it not in fact just her parts that are collectively doing those things?

If we claim that parts and whole are really the same thing, then whatever the whole does, the parts should also do; whatever the whole is, the parts should also be, and vice versa. But if the five aggregates were identified as the self, then there would be five selves at once, since the aggregates are five. It is just as when someone says, "These five socks are red." For that statement to be true, each individual sock has to be red. So too, each aggregate on its own should be the self. The parts and the whole are different because the parts are many and the whole is one. If the parts and the whole were actually the same, then just as there are five parts, there should be five wholes; or, just as there is one whole, there should only be one part.

Can the problem of the plurality of the aggregates be circumvented? Someone says, "I mean the aggregates taken together, not each of them individually. The *collection* of the aggregates is the self." When my hand is in pain, I may quite properly think, "I am in pain." If someone sticks a pin in my finger, they stick a pin in me. But this close relationship between aggregates and self does not mean my aggregates, individually or collectively, are me. The aggregates appear to the ordinary person as mine, not me. If a raindrop falls on my head, it falls on me. They are my aggregates, are they not? Just as a person says, "my house" or "my cow" to refer to possessions outside her continuum of body and mind, so too may she equally say, "my back," "my memory," or "my body and mind" to refer to things within her own entity. That body and mind are mine is adequate reason to establish that they are not me, individually or collectively. Otherwise me and mine become hopelessly confused; how can something be both at once?

The parts belong to the whole; the whole has many parts. It is fair to say, "The whole possesses the parts," just as when someone says, "California possesses a salubrious climate, a long coastline, and two deep water ports," for example. Thus the same can be said of the self possessing the aggregates. Indeed the Tibetan words for part and whole literally mean "part" and "part possessor." If we try to equate the collection of parts with the self, the collection of parts would then have to possess itself, being both that which possesses and that which is possessed. How can anything possess itself? This is unheard of. When I possess something, it becomes mine, my own, not me.

The parts or the collection of parts of the self are the basis in dependence upon which the self arises; the self depends on its parts to be what it is. We depend on our legs to get to the shops and on our hands to prepare our food, just as a tree depends on its roots to stand upright and on its leaves to absorb carbon dioxide. For this reason also, the parts cannot be identical with the self. Something cannot depend on itself any more than it can possess itself. As we have seen, y depends on x because if x did not exist, y would not. A dependent relationship exists between x and y only if x and y are different from each other.

Similarly, we can see that since the self is made up of the parts that compose it, those parts cannot be identical with the whole. Otherwise the self would have to be composed of itself. How could that be? It is meaningless to say that an egg is composed of an egg or concrete is composed of concrete.

The problems of trying to equate the parts with the whole do not end here. If we observe our mind as we go about our life, we apprehend a series of thoughts, experiences, perceptions, and moods. But this series of moments, i.e., parts, of mind cannot be what thinks about my mother when I think about her at a particular time. What about when I look back over a whole lifetime, thinking, "I have had a varied life"? My mind was there for every moment of those accumulated years, but that collection of thoughts, perceptions, and moods was not there in each moment. At any particular moment, there was just one thought, perception, or mood, not the whole series. Thus, even though my mind extends over all its parts without being an entity distinct from them, that does not mean it is simply the equivalent of all its parts.[4]

Furthermore, such a continuum of mind is just as empty as the person imputed in dependence on it. The non-Consequentialist Buddhist schools ascribe a more fundamental mode of being to mind and the other aggregates—substantial existence as opposed to imputed existence. They say that identifying a phenomenon such as mind, form, or blue does not rely on the identification of some other phenomenon. On the other hand, identifying a more complex phenomenon, such as a person or summer, does rely on the identification of some other phenomenon, such as a part. The first type of phenomenon substantially exists. The second type only imputedly exists. But this distinction evaporates when exposed to the Consequentialist analysis. The mind is there solely on the strength of its parts, imputed in dependence on them, in the same way that a person is imputed in dependence on his aggregates and the generality "fruit" is imputed in dependence on its individual instances of bananas and apples. Just as we see fruit on the table merely by virtue of seeing bananas and apples there, so I am only aware of my mind by virtue of my awareness of individual moods and passing moments of perception or conception.

As with instances, so with parts; as with spatial parts, so with temporal ones; among these components or extra to them, no self-sustaining essence that makes a phenomena inherently established is to be found. Instead we find just the opposite, one thing's entire dependence on another. All phenomena have parts of some kind. However minute the components of an atom, they always prove to be divisible. However brief a moment of time, there are always shorter divisions of time within it, even if we have no instrument fine enough to actually measure them. Permanent phenomena such as emptiness and uncaused space are no different. They can be divided according to location if nothing else: there is uncaused space in the East, uncaused space in the West, uncaused space within a cup, uncaused space within a jar, and so forth. All phenomena are guaranteed one form of dependent relationship: dependence on their parts.

Doubting Buddha's declaration that nothing has any inherent mode of existence, wrestling with his proclamation that everything that exists is merely imputed there by the configuring mind, we search again and again for some existence from the object's own side. Seeking the inherently established object, we examine every possible candidate and we investigate every possible location. All are found wanting.

All objects have parts, but an inherently established object could not depend on its parts. In order for an object to have parts but not depend on them, it would either have to be absolutely identical with them—but it is one and they are many—or else it would have to be completely separate from them—but then it could not be made up of them and they could not share in its nature. Where else could an inherently established essence be hiding? We are left face to face with the mere absence of such an objective mode of subsistence. This is the voidness, the emptiness, that our wisdom mind must absorb into and fuse with in direct, single-pointed meditation. The resultant wisdom is the ultimate wisdom; the final view; the vision that bestows peace; the powerful, actual antidote that purifies all the poison of the afflictions and all the contagion of the obstructions.

With insight into emptiness, nirvana is attainable. Combined with universal altruism, it leads all the way to buddhahood. Without it, there is no hope. If things were not empty, there would simply not be any path to freedom.

16 Inherent being has no reverse,
    you taught. So, if things had such being,
    nirvana could not happen nor
    could fabrications be reversed.

As we saw with the example of fire mentioned earlier, nothing that
has inherent being can be affected by any cause or condition. *Nirvana*
literally means "gone beyond sorrow," but there is no way that sorrow
could ever be removed and no way the mind could ever be purified if
nothing could ever act upon it. Buddhahood would be similarly impossible. All the mental distortions that prevent omniscience, "fabrications,"
would be stuck in the mind forever, with no means to eradicate them.

17 "Thus, absence of inherent being!"
    Within the councils of the wise,
    but who could face this lion's roar
    repeatedly resounding forth?

18 "Dependent on this, this occurs":
    All versions of this well accord
    with not the least inherent being.
    What need to say they do not clash?

19 "Arising in dependence then
    is cause for no dependence on
    extremist views." For these fine words
    your speech is unexcelled, O Lord.

20 "These all are void of essence" and
    "From this arises this effect."
    These two discernments mutually
    are not opposed, for each helps each.

21 What is there more astonishing
    and what more wonderful than this?
    So praising you on this account
    is praise indeed; no other is.

6. Mere Imputation

H AVING MADE the marvelous equivalence of dependent arising and emptiness of inherent being shine forth in a series of verses, Tsongkhapa once again draws attention in the middle of his *Praise* to those whose reasoning is muddled and whose vision is incomplete.

22 That those who nurse ill will for you,
    as slaves of ignorance, should find
    the sound of "no inherent being"
    unbearable is no surprise.

It is not so surprising that those outside the Buddhist fold, who have little understanding of dependent relativity, are ill disposed toward and reject what dependent relativity is supposed to prove—no inherent existence.

23 Arising in dependence being
    most treasured of your speech, when some
    accept it but can't bear the call
    of voidness—then I am surprised.

What Tsongkhapa finds unexpected is that followers of Buddha, who have studied dependent arising and declare that they accept it as highly precious, should also spurn emptiness, its natural consequence. Buddha taught explicitly about emptiness in the *Perfection of Wisdom Sutras*. The response of some of the lower schools is to deny that these discourses were actually delivered by Buddha and to say that the great clarifier of this stream of teaching, Nagarjuna, does not deserve to be considered a proponent of Buddhist tenets. Others accept the *Perfection of Wisdom Sutras* as Buddha's word but call them interpretable rather than definitive, meaning they should not be taken at face value. They believe the intended meaning is different from the apparent message of thoroughgoing emptiness.

24 Best door to no inherent being,
   dependent relativity:
   Those nominally for it but
   who grasp at *its* inherent being,

25 Well, how can they be led toward
   the peerless gates through which progressed
   the excellent superior beings,
   the noble path that pleases you?

Thus, though they have arrived at the very gate of understanding of non-inherent existence by taking up the doctrine of dependent relativity, they fail to pass through the gate and follow the path that delights the buddhas. Those who have followed this path to exalted levels are "superior beings." Superiors, or *aryas*, are those who, having first realized emptiness with a conceptual, reasoning mind, have then gone on to realize it with a much more powerful, direct perception. Meditating deeply on emptiness with this direct, single-pointed wisdom is the actual antidote that forever eliminates all the afflictive emotions and their seeds from the mind.

But if all phenomena are devoid of any inherent, objective existence, then how do they validly exist? They are merely imputed by conception. We have seen a few examples of how these other followers of Buddha understand dependent relativity. We have glanced at their basic perspective on arising in dependence on causes and on parts, and we have seen how they accept that some phenomena are imputedly existent and reject the self-sufficiency of persons, though we have shown nothing of the great variety of views that distinguish these schools from one another. We have looked at how the Consequentialists penetrate to the conclusion that objective reality is nowhere to be found. Now we will attempt to suggest what valid mode of existence a Consequentialist does ascribe to phenomena when asserting them to be merely imputed by conception rather than established by way of their own entity.

If we can posit the valid mode of existence, we will be able to cut off the false, though it is said that this subtlest mode of dependent arising, dependence on being merely imputed by conception, does not become entirely clear until after we have realized emptiness. "Merely" in "merely imputed" for the Consequentialists specifically eliminates inherent existence. Therefore the Consequentialist version of imputation is more radical and thoroughgoing than that of the other schools. The latter would, as it were, have their cake and eat it too, accepting that certain phenomena are imputed while clinging to their inherent existence all the same.

We impute an object in dependence on a basis of imputation. Think of someone we know approaching from a distance. First we see a smudge of red. When it draws a little nearer, we impute "Tibetan monk" in dependence on that red form, understanding that someone, a monk wearing red, is coming. When he approaches nearer still, we see a familiar stoop of the shoulders or cheerful smile, and we recognize that it is the abbot who is arriving. In this way, we impute "the abbot" in dependence on the visual aspects of his form aggregate. The red shape is the basis for our imputation of "monk" and the red shape and the stoop of the shoulders or cheerful expression are the basis for our imputation of "abbot." Note the causal sequence: we identify the basis of imputation, which then elicits the thought of the object we impute.

Dispelling Objections

We are now in a position to answer the qualms raised by our hypothetical debater in chapter 3, where he used the examples of an actor projected on film and a house seen in a dream to counter the Consequentialists' complete dismissal of objective existence.

First we will restate the objections using two more examples. Picture a man walking in his garden at dusk. He sees a winding shape, half hidden in the grass. In reality, it is a piece of rope, but he panics, thinking he is about to tread on a snake. But there is nothing more than the appearance of a snake to his mind that he has projected out there. Consequentialists say that an actual snake is very similar to this imaginary snake, in that an actual snake is also merely imputed, also lacking any identity as a snake from its own side. Do not the Consequentialists therefore have to accept the absurdity that, by their own tenets, the imagined snake is an actual snake since they have no valid means to discriminate between the two? If we followed the Consequentialist way of looking at things, then wherever we posited a snake there would have to be one!

Compare dream experiences with experiences of the waking state. Since both sets of experiences are merely projected by the mind and have no true existence, no distinction can be drawn between them in terms of whether they are valid or not. If, for example, a fully ordained monk, who has strict vows against killing, dreamed that he deliberately murdered someone and rejoiced in having done so, would he not have broken his root vow against homicide? In his dream he only killed a merely imputed person, a mere appearance to his mind, but so what? The Consequentialists would have us believe that even a person we kill while we are in the waking state has no mode of being other than as a mere imputation by conception, with nothing from that person's own side to authenticate his appearance to our mind.

In fact, these questions were posed a long ago. The query about killing in a dream is recorded in the sutras as having been put to Buddha himself, while the question about the rope and the snake was dealt with by Nagarjuna.

When our opponent hears the Consequentialists' assertion that all things are merely imputed, to the point that there is nothing left from the object's own side, he assumes that this signifies that all phenomena are merely imaginary, as if to delineate something as a mere imputation denies its existence altogether except as some conjured-up figment of the imagination. But we can distinguish between valid and invalid types of imputation. Going back to our example of the American flag, whoever chose that design could easily have chosen another pattern and color scheme that in the end would have served the purpose just as well. In that sense, the choice was purely arbitrary. Meanwhile, we have all established in our personal conceptual scheme a convention such that when that pattern appears before our mind, the thought, "That's the American flag," is triggered. This connection is something we trained ourselves to make, helped by a teacher or an illustrated book. If anyone pointed at the design of three horizontal stripes of orange, white, and green with a spoked wheel in the center and said, "Look, the U.S. flag," we would shake our heads and reply, "Don't get confused; that's the Indian national flag."

There is nothing inherently American flag-ish about that particular combination of stripes and stars, red, white, and blue. All of us just agree to see that particular design in that particular way, positing "U.S. flag" out there, from our side. But that hardly gives anyone the license to claim any old design he likes as the design of the flag of the United States. Anyone doing so requires forbearance for being a simpleton or invites ridicule for being a buffoon. So we can easily see that mere imputation has its rules too. It is not a case of "anything goes."

Conventional Existence

We associate the meaning "U.S. flag" with that particular design through custom, in conformity with a commonly accepted convention. It is a meaning ascribed by the mind only. This is conventional existence as opposed to ultimate or inherent existence, and it is the valid kind of existence that all phenomena have. But as our flag example suggests, to qualify as conventionally existent, it is not enough to merely appear to mind and be apprehended by one or more sentient creatures. The world would not be flat just because the majority of people thought it was.

In the case of the rope-snake, if the person who thinks the rope is a snake takes a second, closer look, he will see that it does not accord with the convention "snake." He will know the rope for what it is, a rope. If prodded, it does not tense or twitch. It has no life. There is no actual relationship between it and a snake at all, only a certain similarity of appearance in poor light. The subsequent perception, of a piece of rope lying in the grass, establishes that the former one, of the rope as a snake, was mistaken. Seeing the rope as a snake was wrong, just as assuming the world is flat would be.

Such an investigation does nothing to undermine our perception of a snake imputed in dependence on a snake's aggregates. When we check up, on top of the sinuous, legless shape that we first noticed, we find all the things the rope lacks: at one end a head with a mouth and eyes and at the other a tapering tail, also smooth scaly skin, and an ability to slither along the ground; in other words, the characteristics that define a genuine snake. In this case, the slender form, looped in the grass, that in appearing to mind causes snake to appear and the snake that our mind posits there in that place are, as the basis of imputation and the object imputed, very much the same entity. If that slender shape moves, the snake does. If we touch it, we touch the snake. But none of those characteristics in dependence on which a snake is validly imputed either individually or collectively are the snake, and each of them in turn is no more than merely imputed.

The way an ordinary person unversed in philosophy might distinguish between a proper pistol and a child's plastic toy gun is quite sufficient. The latter does not feel like a gun in the hand. The materials it is made of are too weak to shoot lethal bullets. Such a person does not have to assure herself of some singular, ultimate, metaphysical fact of inherently established gun-ness, present in the former and absent in the latter, in order to tell the difference between the two. The same is true of the two different appearances of snake to mind: we can understand that one is in accord with the facts and one is mistaken without it coming down to one being ultimately or inherently established as a snake and the other not.

Likewise, in the case of the dream murder, however real the victim appears to be to the sleeping monk for the duration of the dream, he turns out not to possess the defining characteristics of a person, born at a certain time and place, able to think for himself, able to accumulate karma. Thus the monk in the example does not accumulate the negative deed of killing a person. An actual person, a person seen in a dream, the film image of a person, and the reflection of a person in a mirror, from the point of view of their appearing to be people but not existing from their own side as such, are all the same; but from the point of view of the way ordinary objects are understood and the terminology conventionally used for them, there is all the difference in the world.

The Subtlest Level of Dependent Arising

We can now summarize the differences between the lower schools and the Consequence school concerning the way in which we impute the self. The aggregates are the basis of imputation of the self. The meaning of the self being imputed in dependence on the aggregates is that the self only appears as an object of mind in dependence upon one or more of the aggregates appearing.

The lower schools say that the basis of imputation must be substantially existent and that the self, the object imputed, must exist from the side of the basis of imputation. Their mode of imputation is like someone taking a rope *to be* a snake, in the sense that when they impute the self, they think that something from the side of the aggregates *is* the self. The Consequentialists say that nothing substantially exists; the basis of imputation itself is also merely imputed by conception. They say that the self is not found either amongst the aggregates or separate from them. Think of how we impute a snake in dependence on a snake's head poking out of a narrow hole. We do not take the snake's head *to be* a snake. Similarly when we think "self" in dependence on one or more of the aggregates, nothing from the side of the aggregates whatsoever is the self.

When we mistakenly think a patterned rope is a snake, the snake that arises to mind in the place of the rope is just an appearance of such to the mind that grasps the rope to be a snake, merely posited out there by that mind. Similarly, when we correctly think "I" in dependence on the aggregates, the "I" that arises to that mind is no more than an appearance posited there by that mind.

Understanding the types of selflessness identified by the lower schools helps us to realize the subtler emptiness that the Consequence school asserts. Likewise, an exploration of other versions of imputation is a helpful stepping stone to understanding the Consequentialist explanation of how objects that are utterly devoid of inherent existence nevertheless conventionally exist by being merely imputed by conception. The Consequentialist explanation is more radical and more challenging, but it is the one that passes the test of plain reasoning.

As a further illustration of how the conventions of people's own minds, rather than an object's inherently established nature, determine what we see, we can take the example of a table. A baby who has not yet developed the concept "table" lies on the floor and gazes in fascination at the play of color and shadow across a table's angles and surfaces, his fresh mind deeply absorbed in those colors and shapes above him but ever oblivious to the fact that he is looking up at what we know as a table. Big sister and others play with baby, jogging him up and down on the upper flat surface, showing him and telling him how they are putting their books, Daddy's dinner, and the sewing machine on the table, encouraging baby to see things their way. Eventually the penny drops and the baby adds a new category, another pigeonhole, to his conceptual scheme—raised flat board, suitable to sit at—which, let us say, is the meaning of "table." It is not that he necessarily understands the word "table." It may just be the meaning he establishes at this stage.

Henceforth, when those lights and shadows that the baby previously enjoyed simply as an entrancing visual spectacle appear, they cause "table" to arise to his mind, and he apprehends a table in that place. In dependence upon that play of light and shade, he imputes "table." They signify that table to him now. Until that happens, although big sister and others may see baby bumping his head on the table, from the perspective of the baby's own mind, there is no table. If we could make an inventory of all the items in the baby's world as he conceives it at that time, "raised flat board, suitable to sit at" would not figure in it.

The baby was a single individual who had no table in his world, but it is not difficult to imagine a whole community in the same situation. It is becoming rare now, but not so many years ago there were tribes that had a minimum of material possessions, living largely unadulterated, traditional lives isolated from the materially overdeveloped world. Imagine one such community dwelling deep in the rainforest, their only furniture simple woven fiber mats to sleep on and a log for a seat or a pillow, no raised flat surfaces to put things on and hence no notion of table in their conceptual system. A table then turns up. It falls unnoticed off the back of a truck carrying a survey party of geologists. One of the tribe, straying far outside home territory while hunting, finds it and brings it home. What is it? Who knows? Eventually a handy use is found for it, as a fruit-picking stand. It is very convenient for these rather short people to stand on when picking their favorite berries from the tree. For us it is a table, for them a fruit-picking stand. What it is depends entirely on how it is seen, how it is designated.

Finally, what if the concept "table" never figured in anybody's mental inventory at all in the past, present or future? There is no privileged, knowing observer whatsoever now, and nobody who thinks to pull up a log to a fruit-picking stand and use the latter to support his calabash of beer as he sits there and takes his ease. In this event, table would not exist at all. If there is no conception of table there is no table. Only by figuring in someone's conceptual scheme and being posited out there can a table exist, having no inherent reality of its own. This is just as true for natural phenomena as it is for manmade objects like tables.

There is nothing that is not merely imputed by mind. Simple colors, sounds, and smells, mind itself, emptiness, the truths of the path, and buddhahood are no exceptions. This is the hardest level of dependent relativity to understand. The next verse reveals a complication that might deceive the unwary:

26   Inherent being does not rely
       and is unmade. The relative
       relies, is made; upon one base,
       how do these not just contradict?

All phenomena are included within "the relative." Whether permanent or impermanent, whether a conventional truth like a radio or a person or an ultimate truth like the emptiness of inherent existence of a radio or a person, all are relative; all are dependently related arisings. All phenomena are reliant, or contingent on other phenomena, as short upon long, a sweeper on the act of sweeping, a car on its engine, and the emptiness of a radio on the radio. And all phenomena are "made" or fabricated: impermanent phenomena by their causes, and both permanent and impermanent by the consciousness that imputes them. Anything inherently existent, on the other hand, would be completely isolated. Nothing could bring it into being. Nothing could be related to it in any way, since it would derive its being entirely from itself alone. Hence such a thing would be "unmade" and not contingent. So dependent relativity and inherent existence are excluder and excluded. When we establish dependent relativity on any object, its being inherently existent is clearly ruled out.

The line "The relative relies, is made" is open to a misunderstanding, however. The Consequentialists say a conception apprehending a pot imputes that pot. When, as here, imputing is included within the meaning of making or fabricating, it might sound as if that pot is newly established by the conception imputing it, as if that conception were its cause and produced it. This is a confusion. In general, a pot causes the consciousness apprehending it, not the other way around, as, for example, when we enter a room with a pot in it and generate an eye consciousness seeing it on the table. The eye consciousness that sees it in turn induces a conception, thinking, "That's a pot." Moreover, in the Consequentialist analysis, cause and effect always occur in succession, never simultaneously. In the above sequence there are three time periods to note: first there is a pot, then an eye consciousness of it, and finally a conception apprehending it, imputing it. Thus, a pot, such as one fresh from the kiln, may precede the conception apprehending it and be the cause of the conception apprehending it, even though it is imputed by that very conception.

The disease AIDS is a case in point here. AIDS may have begun affecting humans in the early 1900s when the mutant viruses are thought to have emerged. The first properly authenticated case, retrospectively identified by looking over doctors' records, occurred in 1959, but the disease was not defined and named until 1982, and the virus that causes it was not isolated until 1984.[5] Was not this dreadful disease in existence before it was imputed, even though it only exists by virtue of being imputed?

No phenomenon has any identity that does not rely upon the configuring activity of mind, but there is great difficulty in realizing the truth of this conclusion. Although we ourselves set up the convention in our own mind so that when that particular shape or play of light arises to mind, then "table" arises to mind, we nevertheless deceive ourselves at that very moment into grasping that the table exists from its own side, without being merely posited there by a mind implementing a scheme of interpretation.

> 27   What things dependently arise,
>   thereby though free forever from
>   inherent being, appear that way,
>   all like illusions then, you said.

Buddha did not say that all phenomena are illusions, only that they are "like" illusions. Buddha did not say everything we see around us is completely illusory like a snake seen in the place of a rope at dusk, seen only by a consciousness befuddled by ignorance. Trees, houses, and bicycles exist. We are just mistaken about the way they exist. A mirage appears as water, but it is not water; it is just a mirage. Similarly, conventionally existent things appear to inherently exist but they do not; they just exist conventionally.

Our false view of the world is very much ingrained in us; the appearance of inherent existence is no easy thing to dislodge. Even after we have refuted inherent existence and actually realized emptiness, this appearance will persist, it is said. The mirage of water on a road on a hot day persists in appearing as water, even when we know full well that it is only an optical illusion caused by atmospheric conditions. When learned superior beings arise from direct, single-pointed meditative absorption on emptiness and again engage with the conventional phenomena of the world, those phenomena appear to them as inherently existent. The great difference between those superior beings and people who have not realized emptiness is that the former do not assent to that deceptive appearance, whereas we continue to be duped by it again and again. Buddhas are the only beings who have eliminated not just their grasping at inherent existence, but also the appearance of it to their minds.

Our natural sense that things inherently exist is very strong. Yet reasoning leaves us no choice but to accede to the opposite view, that things are empty. Indeed, it is necessary for things to be empty. They have to be that way in order for the world to operate. Conventional existence, the kind of existence that phenomena do have, is viable and has its own criteria of validity. We have seen that just because all existing things are merely imputed does not mean that anything that is imputed has to exist. When we can see how things are empty of inherent being yet have this other, sufficient mode of existence, we are aligned with the Middle Way, able to steer clear of the two extremes of essentialism and nihilism. Since Buddha's teachings are founded on the wisdom of dependent arising, they show infallibly how to maintain this middle course. Thus Buddha's exposition of the path to enlightenment is unerring, proof against any legitimate criticism.

28   By this we also properly
      may hold to the conclusion that
      no disputant, on genuine grounds,
      can challenge anything you taught.

29   And why? Because by teaching this
      you render distant any chance
      to reify or deprecate
      unseen or seen phenomena.

30   Arising in dependence is
      that path for which your speech is seen
      as peerless. It gives certainty
      all else you taught is valid too.

In these three verses, Tsongkhapa praises dependent arising as the pervading element whose presence renders the whole corpus of Buddha's teachings coherent and logically unassailable, and makes Buddha's path uniquely profound and far-reaching. So wonderful is this teaching of dependent arising that it gives not just confidence but "certainty" that the one who taught it, Buddha, is in all respects an authoritative teacher.

The "seen" or "unseen" phenomena liable to be exaggerated or denied by those stuck in either of the two extremes are, respectively, those objects that are directly manifest to our ordinary sense consciousnesses and the more abstruse objects that we can initially only comprehend through reasoning. Although emptiness is one of those "unseen" phenomena that can initially only be ascertained by reasoning, the reasoning of dependent relativity that establishes it relies on premises that are widely accepted, even by those who have not yet adopted a Buddhist worldview. So powerful in its effects and yet accessible through plain reasoning, an understanding of dependent arising bestows conviction that all of Buddha's teachings are sound, including those on subjects not so easily fathomed by ordinary mortals. It is the outstanding example by which we can judge that all of his teachings point the way to evolution's highest stage.

7. Daily Life

31 You saw things as they are and taught
that well. Your students' troubles then
will all recede away, since they
will halt all defects at the root.

32 Who turn away from what you taught
may long perform austerities,
yet they, fixated on the self,
just summon faults repeatedly.

33 Amazing when the wise perceive
the difference between these two.
Then from the very marrow shall
they not have reverence for you?

34 How much you taught, why speak of that?
Determining but generally
the meaning of a single part
just that bestows a special joy.

THOSE WHO REALIZE and recollect emptiness will cease to assent to any appearance of phenomena as inherently existent. But in spite of that realization, it is said that until they have reached full enlightenment, things will persist in appearing to their minds as they did before. Only Buddha sees things "as they are."

It is very difficult to imagine what that experience must be like. A special feature of Buddha's extraordinary perception is that he is able to see a phenomenon's conventional truth and ultimate truth simultaneously. That is, he can see a pot, a conventional truth, and the emptiness of inherent existence of that pot, its ultimate truth, at the same time. Even people who have realized emptiness directly but who have not reached buddhahood can only observe either the conventional nature or the ultimate one, not both simultaneously.

It is said that Buddha does not see ordinary conventional truths, such as the houses, clouds, and trees of our world, from his own point of view. Rather he knows such phenomena through the way they appear to the minds of ordinary beings. He knows them only by knowing what ordinary beings are experiencing. Such an explanation may well sound inconceivable when we first hear it. It is difficult for our weak understanding to expand to encompass a buddha's surpassing qualities of realization and compassionate action.

Even to conjecture what a realization of emptiness must be like is quite difficult. The best analogy we have is empty space. Both space and emptiness are permanent, so there is no momentary fluctuation occurring. Both are understood only in terms of there being an absence of something else, and both are all-pervasive and open. Uncaused space is defined by its lack of obstruction and contact. Due to this lack, forms that occupy space, such as mountains and bodies, have room to exist in the places they do. Due to there being empty space in a pot, it can be filled with water. This lack of obstruction and contact does not have any positive qualities. The absence of a coin in our hand is similar. Such a phenomenon is only cognized by bringing our idea of a coin to mind, checking whether one is there in our hand, and discovering its absence. In the same way, we can only understand emptiness by first bringing our idea of inherent existence to mind, searching for it, and determining it not to be. Emptiness is a sheer absence, in this case of something that never existed in the first place but that we formerly took for granted. To say that an experience of emptiness is like a vision of light could thus be misleading, in that light, as form, has positive qualities, whereas emptiness is only a state of negation.

The Benefits of Studying Dependent
Arising and Emptiness

There is a story of a monk in Tibet who went about proclaiming that he had realized emptiness. He was asked to describe it, and he said it was like a pigeon. After that he was given the nickname Professor Pigeon! But from what other people say, we can deduce that when one experiences emptiness, one has a very relaxed feeling. Due to our delusions, our mind is in a constant state of agitation, like boiling water. Disturbing states of mind are constantly arising; conceptions and projections bubble up endlessly. When one realizes emptiness, it is as though someone has poured a larger amount of cold water onto that boiling water, which then becomes cool and still. The mind becomes relaxed and clear in a way it never was before.

We should not be discouraged by thinking that emptiness is difficult to realize correctly, for a complete realization of it will "halt all defects at the root." It does not simply bring about the abstract satisfaction of discovering something that happens to be true. As we see in verse 32, without it, even if we practiced asceticism and mortified our bodies as yogis of some other sects do, we would be doing nothing that fundamentally opposed cyclic existence. Buddha himself spent several years practicing austerities in the company of such ascetics before rejecting that as a path to liberation.

A "special joy" arises from assimilating even a small part of Buddha's teachings. Likewise, a simple understanding of some aspects of the doctrine of dependent arising, though not amounting to a realization of emptiness as such, will bring joy by dissolving self-obsession and lightening the heart. Even if we feel we are a long way from Tsongkhapa's level of illumination and insight, contemplating different aspects of dependent arising such as those we have described is a sure way for us to help ourselves and to increase our tolerance and concern for others in our present daily lives.

Considering the ways in which things are dependent on causes is itself a great antidote to the self-centered and self-satisfied attitudes that make us insensitive to the concerns of others and dismissive of their legitimate needs. When we are happy, we do not notice how the kindness of many beings has contributed to our happiness. But when we are down, we lunge for a simplistic explanation that places all the blame on others. We probably all have the tendency to think that whatever good health or excellent knowledge we have has come about through our own care and attention, and that whatever pleasant experiences we enjoy are the deserved fruits of our own hard work.

When we analyze how the good conditions we enjoy arise, we often tend to go no further than some such thought as, "I know how to take care of myself," or, "I put in a lot of effort to be able to afford this." If we go to a restaurant and have a delicious meal, we might think that our ability to do so depends on our own means, on having earned enough money to pay for it. However, if we investigate what being able to eat a meal in a restaurant really depends on, we will see that in fact an enormous amount of effort has to be put in by countless numbers of other beings before we can be served our choice of food. If we are eating rice, just think of all the work of the farmers who plow the land, then plant, irrigate, weed, and finally harvest their crops. Of course all their labor and that of their animals would be in vain if the elements did not cooperate and provide the right amount of sunshine and rain. Then the rice has to be cleaned and hulled and prepared for the table. Then it is distributed to shops and put on sale, requiring yet another network of people. Once the rice has reached the restaurant, the kitchen staff have to work on the final stage of the process of making it fit to eat. The kitchen and the dining room themselves were built through the labor of gangs of people; and the cooks' utensils, the fuel for cooking, and the serving dishes have only become available in dependence on the inventiveness, ingenuity, and effort of another vast number of designers, administrators, salespeople, accountants, factory workers, and miners, all their families and teachers, and so forth.

In McLeod Ganj, India, where His Holiness the Dalai Lama lives in exile, there are a considerable number of restaurants catering largely to the pilgrims, students, and tourists who come there from all over the world. As the number of visitors has increased, so have the hotel and restaurant facilities expanded. Clearly the visitors depend on the restaurants and hotels; the hotel and restaurant workers equally depend on the visitors. As the range of facilities for visitors improves, so are more people tempted to come; as the number of visitors increases, so are more people able to take to the business of selling them food, souvenirs, handicrafts, and books on Buddhism.

Many of the Tibetan shop and hotel owners would say that this situation ultimately rests on the kindness of His Holiness and the Three Jewels—the Buddha, the Dharma, and the Sangha. Such Tibetans are very happy to see these visitors, happy for the economic benefits of course but also for the benefit the visitors can derive from finding out about Buddhism. The visitors are pleased that the facilities in McLeod Ganj are not so bad and that they can get decent food there. They can appreciate the welcome they receive and the cheerfulness of the Indians and Tibetans, and they too can understand that there is mutual benefit in their being there. But if either side were to lapse into a more self-centered way of thinking, such as, "I am the one who built up this restaurant by my hard work," or, "I can eat at this expensive restaurant because I worked hard and saved up a lot of money," then, thinking that their fortunate situation did not depend on others, there would be a danger of a degeneration of this happy feeling and mutual tolerance of each others' foibles.

Another example of the benefits of remembering dependent arising occurs in the following story of a man who was going to market with his yak. As the man was leading the yak along a mountain path, the yak slipped and fell into a narrow place in such a way that it was unable to rise again. So the man made a strong prayer to the buddhas and to Padmasambhava in particular, and by heaving on the rope, he was able to get the yak back on its feet. But instead of thinking about the kindness of the buddhas or the Three Jewels, he set off again on his journey with a very inflated view of his own strength. A little further on, the yak fell down again. This time the man thought he could get the yak back on its feet just by tugging on the rope, without bothering with the prayer, but try as he might, the yak remained stuck, and he could not shift it an inch!

Whatever we undertake, if we remember that our success depends on far more than just our own prowess or wealth, we will be more deeply in touch with the reality of the situation, since the dependent relationships of one phenomenon with others are, in fact, countless. As for the power of prayer, Padmasambhava was one of the first and greatest yogis to spread Buddha's teachings in Tibet, and a prayer supported by strong faith in him can help good karma to ripen at a certain point to bring about a desired result. Just as a child's willingness to learn makes it possible for the teacher to draw out the child's understanding, so too, as in the story, making a prayer can draw out our ability to solve a particular problem at a critical time.

We can transcend limited attitudes and negatively tinged emotions by recollecting causes and conditions in these different ways. Mindfulness of how things depend on parts can also be applied to the same practical end. Through introspection and meditation, we become aware that every time annoyance or meanness threatens to dominate our minds, we made the way open by grasping at ourselves to exist in a self-powered manner. If we act quickly, before the current of that disturbing emotion gathers momentum, we can challenge the exaggerated sense of self that sets it going. If we really exist in this all-of-a-piece, from-our-own-side manner, let us bring this marvelous self into focus. But what happens when we search for it? It disappears.

Where is it? An additional entity, lording it over the parts? The self may control its parts in a sense, but the flow of influence is hardly one-way. Being made up of the parts, the self is not distinct from them, and it is entirely subject to their influence. A self that is in addition to the parts is an impossibility then. Is it found among the parts? But no part or collection of parts can do the work of the whole. The self merely depends on its parts, like a forest on its trees, like a walk to town on the individual steps. When we challenge the objectively existing, all-of-a-piece self to appear for scrutiny, it dissolves into nothing.

Even if we end up with only a suspicion, rather than a clear insight, that the self is actually empty of inherent existence, we are still much better off, in a better humor, with the potential to deal more skillfully with whatever challenges we face, instead of suffocating under the burden of an afflictive emotion. Of course, to be able to activate this process of investigation readily in the heat of the moment, we need to train ourselves well beforehand, when we are meditating in tranquility. Later, when the distorted sense of a self that exists by its own power manifests, we can isolate it straightaway and then quash it with the reasoning of its being dependent on its parts, neither one with them nor separate from them.

We should not be content with seeing this bothersome, exaggerated self temporarily fade away. We should also turn our attention to the aggregates, to root out any sense we have that the aggregates are in some way more substantial or foundational than the self. The aggregates are only imputed in dependence on their parts, and they are just as dependent on the self as it is on them. The relationship is one of mutual dependence, as it always is between parts and whole. For the parts of a bicycle to be there, there must be a bicycle to which they belong. When the so-called parts of a bicycle are scattered over the repair shop's floor, at that point, there is no bicycle. Strictly speaking, there are no parts of a bicycle there either, only the parts of a would-be or future bicycle. If a critic argues that those bits and pieces scattered over the workshop floor are the parts of a bicycle, is that because they could easily become a bicycle? Does it then follow that Prince Charles is King of England because he could easily become King of England? No parts exist without their respective wholes.

Parts and whole each serve as the basis of imputation for the other. Picture that we are standing outside at night somewhere in the country looking down a dark wooded hill when our attention is drawn by two wavering gleams and a roaring sound. After a moment or two of puzzlement, we understand that there is a car coming, as "car" arises to mind in response to the appearance of that combination of visual form and sound. Yet we only recognize those twin gleams of light flickering through the trees as the headlights of a car, and that straining roar coming nearer up the hill as the sound of a car engine, in dependence on our understanding that there is a car approaching. Neither the car nor its parts are apprehended in isolation from one another. Neither is more fundamental or foundational than the other.

This mutual reliance of parts and wholes is like an old man who gets up with the aid of a stick. In order to rise, the old man leans on his stick. The old man is therefore supported by his stick, but at the same time, the stick is supported by the man. Without the man to place the stick in an upright position and hold it there, the stick would be unable to perform the function of bearing the man's weight. All objects only exist to the extent that they participate in these relationships of interdependence with other objects, with parts, with the observing mind. There is no essential bedrock, no primordial ground, no creator god they are traced back to or are guaranteed by.

Countering Attachment

The lower schools' versions of selflessness apply directly to persons. For them phenomena other than persons are selfless only in the weak sense of their not being objects of use of a permanent, unitary, independent self or of a self-sufficient, substantially existent self. The emptiness asserted by the Consequence school applies to all phenomena whatsoever. To thoroughly eliminate the ignorance that is at the root of suffering, we must contemplate that not only ourselves and our aggregates but all the things of this world we use and enjoy are also empty in exactly the same way. This is particularly helpful in dealing with the afflictive emotion of attachment. We cannot feel attachment for a pleasant object unless we have already grasped it to be inherently existent.

For example, when we see an article in a shop window, say a radio or a pair of shoes, at first it will appear to be inherently existent. Such objects may be pleasurable and useful for beings such as us, who are able to listen out on the world with ears attuned to the vibrations of sound and who have such tender toes. It is not that all our artificial comforts and the pleasure we take in the wonders of this world are utterly false. But there is a certain point at which our attraction to an enjoyable object becomes the negative emotion of attachment.

Attachment is the desire to become close to, possess, or not be separated from a person or thing, having exaggerated the good qualities of that object. This contrasts with love, the wish for another being or beings to be happy. Attachment the way we have characterized it here is based on unrealistically high expectations of the object and a desire for pleasure for ourselves. It is not primarily concerned about any other person's happiness. Defined in this way, attachment is wholly a negative emotion, so categorized because it leads to clinging, disappointment, and pain when the object fails to satisfy our exaggerated expectations.

Sometimes the wholesome fondness of, say, a child for her pet dog that she enjoys taking care of is called *attachment*. ("She's very attached to that little dog.") But the delight the child feels in giving comfort and happiness to another creature is not what we mean by *attachment* here. That would be more like love. However, as those mature in worldly relationships may know, love and attachment are often intermingled and difficult to tell apart. Thus as we remark on avoiding the pitfalls of this afflictive emotion, it is easier to stick to examples of attachment to inanimate objects.

When we assent to the appearance of a beautiful or otherwise pleasant object as inherently existent, the object then appears not just pleasurable but inherently pleasurable, a guaranteed source of pleasure. We see its ability to give its owner happiness right there within it. But like any object in this disintegrating world, it is fallible, mutable; in the end, its ability to give happiness is dependent on circumstances. It needs an inordinate amount of looking after, but still it gets scratched, broken, lost, or borrowed by an elder brother who forgets to give it back. We must cut through appearances by recollecting that if it is inherently existent, it should be findable among the parts or separate from them. Because it is neither, and is only dependent on the parts, the appearance of the object's inherently established nature must simply recede away. When we think, "I have just posited the beauty of the object there solely by the power of my own mind," attachment will have no basis.

If we do not counter mara's temptation right at the start, the stream of attachment to the exaggerated object is quickly joined by the stream of attachment to the overblown self—"*I* must have the object so that *I* can be happy"—and then one-sided grasping at happiness for myself or my dear ones supersedes all other considerations. When these two streams unite, attachment becomes terribly strong and hard to disassociate from. In a simple form, we can see this happening in the case of a child sulking for having been refused the soccer ball in the shop window he is fixated upon. In an extreme form, we can see it in the alcoholic reaching for yet another glass. These are two blatant cases where deluded attachment, having invested an object with much more happiness-potential than it can ever provide, makes the person crave the object without concern for others and against his own best interests. We should investigate how often we are tempted to act in the same way.

Once I have acquired my object of desire, it quickly appears to be inherently mine, belonging to me by absolute right, as if the mine-ness resided right there within the object. In fact, it is mine only by virtue of being mentally pigeonholed that way. It is mine only in the sense that I cause it to appear in that way to my mind (and hopefully to others' minds!), positing that mere appearance out there on the object. There is nothing absolute about this type of mine-ness at all, and nothing fixed. Everything we have is borrowed and will have to be handed back presently. Immediately questioning the inherently existent status of the object and the self before attachment to either can gather strength is a primary line of defense against this affliction of unwarranted desire.

Tsongkhapa ends this section of *Praise for Dependent Relativity* on a cautionary note of modesty:

35   Confusion seized my mind, alas.
      Though taking refuge for so long
      in that array of qualities,
      no part of one have I attained.

36   But while life's stream has not yet sunk
      inside the mouth of death itself,
      I count it fortunate to have
      belief in you, however slight.

Though ostensibly he is talking only of himself, Tsongkhapa's remarks are intended as a word of guidance to his disciples. He denies having understood anything or having achieved any aspect of the path to the buddha ground. This is not because that really was the case, as he discloses in verse 51. Rather, his modesty here is for his followers to imitate. Apparently, it is unwise for those with spiritual realizations, especially nascent ones, to tell others less advanced than they are about their attainments. One danger is that others' admiration will lead to pride. Therefore it is better for such a person to mentally contrast her own diminutive achievement with Buddha's and just speak of her own faith in him, even then deprecatingly. Tsongkhapa, on this particular morning, is well able to see exactly why Buddha is worthy of the greatest faith, being the ultimate source of refuge.

We may conclude of Tsongkhapa that, being a supreme teacher, a teacher among teachers, the dangers he counsels against here hardly apply to himself. But even though Tsongkhapa is revered as one of the very greatest scholars and adepts, who reinvigorated and clarified Buddhist doctrine in Tibet and left behind a magnificent corpus of writings of the most penetrating kind, when he is compared to Buddha himself, Buddha's qualities are vaster still. If we stand by the side of a large lake, the expanse of water may seem enormous, but in comparison to it, the waters of the ocean are far wider and still deeper.

8. Fulfillment

37 Of teaching, that of relativity,
   of insight, insight into that: these two
   are like a great subduer, throughout the worlds
   supreme. You saw this well; no others did.

I N THE ORIGINAL Tibetan version of *Praise for Dependent Relativity*, all of the verses through verse 52 except verse 37 have seven-syllable lines. Verse 37 stands out from the flow by having two extra syllables per line. We can suppose the verse is highlighted in this way because it stands as a concise recapitulation of the essential message of the text, namely that the qualities of Buddha that made his appearance in this world system uniquely valuable were his possessing the wisdom of dependent relativity and his teaching of it. Other wise ones preceded Buddha or appeared subsequently, but if they had a deep understanding of dependent relativity, they failed to convey it down the ages to the wider audience; if they were well-known and eloquent teachers, they lacked wisdom, and the full import of dependent relativity eluded them. Tsongkhapa says that having the teachings on dependent arising available together with the wisdom that realizes those teachings is like still enjoying Buddha's presence in our world today.

38 All that you taught starts and proceeds
   from relativity alone,
   and with nirvana as the goal,
   no deed of yours was not for peace.

39 Amazing that your teachings bring
    all those whose ears they reach to peace,
    so who will not hold in esteem
    the preservation of your word?

40 All opposition it destroys;
    no contradiction found within.
    It yields all creatures' dual aims.
    My pleasure in this system grows.

Though the teachings of Buddha are extensive in terms of their thoroughness and the range of subjects they cover, all of them relate directly or indirectly to profound dependent relativity, since this is what makes all the attainments of the path possible, including nirvana, the surpassing state of peace.

The limitations of our present state of mind and the recurring frustrations of this passing round of birth, sickness, aging, and death are not the inevitable, fixed nature of things. Just as pure carbon in an amorphous state may be soft and densely black yet in another manifestation the hardest and most brilliantly reflective of gems, so our mind has the possibility of passing from the muddle of disturbing emotions to a jewel-like state of peace and primordial purity. Our means is Buddha's teachings. Thus there is no question that preserving them is worthwhile.

Tsongkhapa states in verse 40 that Buddha's teachings have "no contradiction found within." However, as we have reviewed a few of the key points of the different tenet systems that have been codified from the sutras, we have noted teachings that appear to be quite contradictory to one another. In one place, Buddha allowed that the self inherently exists, while in another, he refuted inherent existence with abundant reasons. Not everyone is ready for the deepest teaching. A rather different teaching may be suitable for a beginner than for an adept. So Buddha taught a variety of approaches suitable for leading beings of all different aptitudes to an unerring understanding of the full meaning of dependent relativity.

There was a king called Ajatashatru who seized power in the kingdom of Magadha, a region of India where Buddha often wandered and taught. So evil was the king that he killed his own father in order to gain the throne for himself. He indirectly brought about the death of his mother also. His way of life was utterly contrary to that which Buddha advocated. He developed a strong antipathy toward Buddha, and he tried to kill him, too, by sending a mad elephant charging toward the place where Buddha was teaching in the hope that he might be trampled to death. King Ajatashatru rejected the idea of highly evolved beings that could be objects of refuge, the necessity of practicing virtue, and the existence of past and future lives. His mother and father, however, had shown great faith in Buddha, and both had led lives of extraordinary virtue. The father had spoken to his son many times about Buddha's teachings.

After the father died, he appeared in a vision to his son. Ajatashatru's vision shocked him to the core, and his former skeptical outlook was abruptly overturned. He saw there were past and future lives and became very afraid of the future consequences of having killed his father and allowing his mother to die of grief. The king wondered whether to go to Buddha and throw himself at Buddha's feet. Buddha was aware of all this and knew that if he told the king how intensely negative the act of parricide was, then the king would be plunged into such a crisis of despair that he might even die from it. Buddha therefore understood that, on this occasion, telling the bald truth would not be beneficial.

According to one account, the king, full of inner torment, passed by where Buddha was teaching. In the king's presence, Buddha said that in order to practice Dharma, the first thing one should do is to kill one's mother and father. Then one should kill the king of the kingdom, his two chief ministers, all his attendants, and then all the servants of the attendants. The king was extremely fascinated by this teaching and simply amazed that Buddha should have taught it. With the overwhelming anxiety about his actions thus diverted, the king was able to think more freely. Back in his palace, he pondered what Buddha had said. He understood Buddha to be a person who had abandoned violence in all its forms, yet here he was teaching that one should kill people in order to find liberation from suffering.

The king eventually came to understand that the superficial level of the teaching was merely a device to snare the attention of a mind distraught to the point of madness. The real meaning of the teaching that one should kill one's father and mother was that one should eradicate the two root causes of cyclic existence. Ignorance and karma are what impel rebirth in cyclic existence. In this way, they are like the father and mother from whom all beings in cyclic existence are born. Killing the king of the kingdom refers to eliminating defiled consciousness. The mind is the instigator of actions, so within the context of a person, the mind is like a king in a kingdom. These three elements, ignorance, karma, and consciousness, are the first three of the twelve links of dependent relativity. The two chief ministers that must be killed can either be interpreted as two more of the twelve links, or as the two extremes, the views of essentialism and nihilism. The royal attendants refer to the rest of the twelve links, and the servants of the attendants refer to all the objects in cyclic existence.

As King Ajatashatru deduced all of this, a great faith in Buddha awakened in him, and he went on to become one of the major patrons of Buddhism of his day, as his father had been before him. There are other explanations of what exactly Buddha meant by father, mother, king, and so on here, but the general message is the same: we can overcome cyclic existence by bringing the production of the twelve links of dependent relativity to a halt. This is just one example of how different teachings that may appear contradictory on the superficial level are resolved when their full import becomes clear.

"All creatures' dual aims" that Buddha's teaching fulfills are the goals of oneself and others. Buddha is someone who has not just achieved peace for himself but who has also perfected his capacity to bring others to peace. He does not just teach the path of individual escape to one's own personal serenity but also the stages of training that result in full enlightenment, where one has the fullest capacity to benefit others. Verse 41 indicates just how long and difficult this latter path can be:

41　For countless ages for its sake
　　you gave away repeatedly

at times your body or your life,
the ones you loved, a mass of wealth.

The bodhisattva must accumulate a vast store of virtues by serving the welfare of others over an immense series of lifetimes.

Tsongkhapa's Path to Awakening

In the culminating section of *Praise for Dependent Relativity* before the final dedicatory verses, Tsongkhapa strikes a more personal note, revealing some of his own experiences in trying to follow this very path of the bodhisattva. No individual dramatic acts of self-sacrifice are revealed, but a string of images illuminates the picture of a life of unswerving dedication. They describe the uplift of energy and protection from sorrow that flow from pure faith in Buddha and the blissful relief of finally coming to the actual quintessential meaning of the teachings, which is the experience that inspired the composition of this text. If anyone should ask about Tsongkhapa's efforts on behalf of others, we have only to point to his teachings, such as this *Praise* itself, as evidence of his lifelong devotion to helping others by transmitting Buddha's speech in a critically examined, purified, and revitalized form, and thus inspiring others to follow the path that leads beyond sorrow.

42   And when you saw its qualities,
     this doctrine drew your heart, as does
     a hook a fish. Sad fate for me
     not hearing it from you yourself.

43   In virtue of this sorrow's strength
     just like a mother's mind that is
     intent upon a darling child,
     may my mind never deviate.

44   And, dwelling on your speech, I think
     of you, O Teacher, blazing with

the glories of the signs and marks,
enhaloed by a radiant light,

45 In your sweet voice discoursing thus
and thus. As moon rays, fever's pangs,
O Sage, your likeness brings relief
in just appearing to my mind.

Tsongkhapa describes how Buddha, while still a wandering, migrating being, is captivated by the good qualities of the Dharma like a fish hooked tight. Tsongkhapa feels a bereft sadness at not having been there to hear the teachings from Buddha himself, but he brings this sorrow into the path by using it to impel himself to concentrate undistractedly on the training, like a mother whose dear child is always at the center of her thoughts.

Through Tsongkhapa's great faith, Buddha appears to his mind's eye, splendidly arrayed, discoursing in a melodious voice. A circle of disciples was present when Buddha turned the wheel of Dharma in person. Tsongkhapa visualizes Buddha before him as if he were one of those fortunate ones and receives blessings that dissolve his sorrows. In an image we can imagine was imported from India to the cooler land of Tibet, Tsongkhapa compares these blessings to moonbeams that are able to soothe the torment of heat. In a country like India, the sun can be oppressively hot, but when the moon comes out in the evening, its rays are said to have a pacifying, cooling effect, a relief especially to those suffering from fever.

46 So marvelous and excellent
a system this, yet those who had
no mastery, like *balbaja*,
were tangled up in every way.

47 I recognized their plight and so
I followed in the masters' steps
and your intended meaning sought
repeatedly with greatest zeal.

48   I studied many texts, our own
      and those of others, at this time.
      My mind was yet repeatedly
      all baffled in a net of doubts.

Verses 42–45 speak of Tsongkhapa's inner inspiration, the strength he drew from direct contact with the energy of the buddhas in meditation. Verses 46–48 reveal his assiduous dedication to the process of studying Buddha's doctrine. The buddhas in their fully enlightened form are only hidden from us because of the dimness of our own minds. If, in stillness, we can withdraw the mind from worldly distractions and open up to a purer level, we will soon feel the dawn of inspiration of enlightened energy, and by pursuing a precise understanding through study, we can further awaken and direct our own buddha potential. These two approaches mutually reinforce each other. If we follow the order suggested by the verses, encouraging the enlightened energy to arise in our minds by drawing our attention inward and placing it on a visualized image of Buddha, such as in the act of taking refuge, then it becomes far easier to study and contemplate the subject of emptiness.

Asanga, Nagarjuna, Bhavaviveka, Buddhapalita: these are great names in the history of Buddhist thought, outstanding minds who extracted from Buddha's words different philosophical systems suited to the people of a particular era or culture. It is no easy matter after centuries of debate and refinement to determine which interpretation embodies Buddha's definitive view, the wisdom that definitively liberates. It's no wonder then that Tsongkhapa found many people's ideas all tangled up "like *balbaja*." *Balbaja* is the Sanskrit name for a type of grass (*Eleusine indica*) that grows in densely intertwined clumps. If we, like Tsongkhapa, develop doubts and have many questions to ask, this is a favorable sign, showing that we have the curiosity and application to make our own attempts to ascend these peaks of wisdom.

Buddha set forth the highest view, but it is said that only those of very sharp intelligence can understand Buddha's ultimate intent by studying this view alone. To passively acquiesce in the highest view merely because our teacher says it is the highest is not something even those who incline to Buddhism of the heart rather than Buddhism of the head should really be content with. It is almost as if Buddha deliberately delivered teachings open to different levels of interpretation in order to provoke his followers into debating one side of a question against another. In doing so, we will refine and sharpen our minds to the point where we can begin to understand the truth's vital subtleties, allowing us to arrive at the correct conclusions actively through our own power of reasoning. Thus the truth will not remain as a dogma to which we feebly assent but will become internalized as the powerful force it should be, vanquishing confusion, bestowing clarity, efficacious for good.

In verses 47 and 48, Tsongkhapa explains how he ransacked the writings of other Buddhist and non-Buddhist schools, only to be left dissatisfied and unconvinced by their presentations. Nonetheless, his study of their views and his identification of their defects was an entirely suitable preparation for his deeper soundings of the Consequentialist view. Then, in one of the most beautiful metaphors of the verses, he describes how he finally entered into the ultimate view in reliance upon the texts of Nagarjuna and Chandrakirti. Tsongkhapa wrote the *Praise* out of his own thorough realization of the final view, and not forgetting the kindness of his own personal teachers, he acknowledges those two geniuses of Indian Buddhism as his guides on the journey to that fulfillment. Nagarjuna blazed the trail to be followed by upholding the view that emptiness and dependent relativity are utterly noncontradictory. Chandrakirti, whose name means "as famous as the moon," drew forth the import of Nagarjuna's texts and explained the distinctive features of the Consequentialist version of the Middle Way view.

49 When through the lama's kindness I
    beheld the grove of all the texts
    of Nagarjun, foretold to show
    just how your highest vehicle shuns

50 The extremes of being and nonbeing both,
    made bloom by white light-garlands of
    the speech of glorious Moon, whose sphere
    waxed full of stainless wisdom sails

51   Unchecked the heaven of sacred speech,
     dispels the heart's extremist gloom,
     outshines the stars of erring talk,
     O then my mind arrived at rest.

Nagarjuna's texts are likened to the flowers in a garden that only blossom at night by the light of the moon (*chandra*). Chandrakirti, the clearest and most reliable Indian commentator on Nagarjuna's elegantly terse and often paradoxical stanzas, is likened to the moon that bathes the garden in the white light of wisdom and causes the flowers of Nagarjuna's text to open and reveal the exquisite beauty of their true meaning. Earlier Tsongkhapa compared the blessings that came from visualizing Buddha to the soothing radiance of the moon. Here he describes how he finds final relief when the moonbeams of pure wisdom enter his heart and dissolve the melancholy of false views.

Six verse treatises by Nagarjuna explaining emptiness and setting forth the Middle Way view are often taken together as a set. Their emphasis is strongly on refuting clinging to inherent existence, to which the Buddhist scholars of his day were apparently addicted. Opponents of this renowned, not to say legendary, philosopher and practitioner who were unable to discriminate between no existence and no inherent existence were quick to accuse him of denying the existence of phenomena altogether. Chandrakirti replied to these critics by setting forth not just the way in which phenomena are devoid of inherent existence but also the way in which they do nonetheless conventionally exist. Having exposed the error of acquiescing in the illusion of inherent existence, he dwells on the dependently arisen mode of existence phenomena do have. His *Supplement to the "Middle Way"* remains the best introduction to Nagarjuna's thought.

Among Tsongkhapa's contemporaries in Tibet there was plenty of disagreement about how exactly the Middle Way view should be understood. Many had a tendency to overemphasize emptiness at the expense of dependent relativity. Tsongkhapa received more than one vision of his supernal guru, Manjushri, the deity who is the embodiment of all the buddhas' wisdom, symbolized by the flaming sword he holds aloft. In answer to Tsongkhapa's request for guidance, Manjushri directed him to rely on Chandrakirti's *Supplement to the "Middle Way"* as a faultless exposition by one who had complete understanding. Tsongkhapa in turn composed many works that have helped keep the ancient flame of this profoundest wisdom burning for the generations who have come after him. His life was short compared to Buddha's or Nagarjuna's, but he left a treasure store of commentaries and expositions of the scriptures behind. So just as he praises Buddha, we should praise him, not for his realizations alone, but also for the eloquence and skill with which he passed on his discriminating knowledge to others.

52　Of all the deeds, the deed of speech
　　was best; of that, of this, and so,
　　with this your reason, learned ones,
　　remember the Enlightened One.

Tsongkhapa singles out Buddha's speech, his teaching, as his supreme deed, because this is the action that has benefited sentient beings the most. "Of that," speech, the teaching "of this," dependent relativity, is the most precious, for which we may commemorate the Awakened One above all else.

Buddha is credited with having performed many miracles. In one well-known account, the adepts of some other Indian paths of knowledge argued with Buddha some time after his enlightenment and engaged him in a legendary contest of magical powers. The site of this competition was Shravasti in northern India. Buddha won the contest, but where are those magical emanations and dazzling shows now? When we see paintings of the miracles that Buddha performed, we may wonder whether these events really happened. In any case, those fabulous deeds are lost in the past, but his teachings are still very much with us, preserved in a pure form of words and in the minds of those with realizations.

Dedication

53 As follower of this teacher I went forth,
and not ill versed in the Subduer's speech,
I strove in yoga practice as a monk,
such my devotion for that mighty seer.

54 The kindness of the lama brought me to
the foremost teacher's teachings, so too I
this virtue dedicate as cause that all
be cared for by a holy spiritual friend.

55 Our Helper's teachings till the world's end be
not shaken by the wind of evil thoughts,
and be it ever full with those who find
trust in the Teacher, knowing what he taught.

56 May we, no moment's faltering, all our births,
though life or body be the cost, maintain
dependently arising's suchness, this,
the noble way the Sage made manifest.

57 The best of guides, through countless trials, stressed this
to be the essence and let day and night
pass in examining whatever ways
by which what he achieved can be increased.

58 Who strive this way with pure and high resolve,
you, Brahma, Indra, worldly guardians and
protectors, Mahakala and the like,
without distraction always lend your aid.

Six remaining verses bring *Praise for Dependent Relativity* to a conclusion with the customary dedication of merits. Tsongkhapa dedicates the merit of composing these stanzas to the most beneficial ends. This last group of verses once more employs a nine-syllable line in Tibetan, a relaxation from the intensity of the shorter seven-syllable lines that culminated in Tsongkhapa's account of how he opened to the final view, modestly described by way of his singular praise of Nagarjuna and Chandrakirti.

Verse 53 is the briefest résumé of the author's personal journey. He determined to forsake the world and so he "went forth" from the house-holder's life to the homeless life by becoming a monk. Then he made no slight study of Buddha's teachings, and with joyful diligence he put the teachings into practice and sought their inner meaning.

Tsongkhapa's involvement with the teachings would not have occurred without the kind guidance of a personal mentor. Tsongkhapa again reminds the reader who might become interested in Buddhism of the supreme importance of the lama or spiritual guide. It cannot all be learned from books! Thus he prays that the virtue of composing this work may act as a cause for all beings to come under the indispensable care of such a mentor.

Next, in verse 55, Tsongkhapa prays for the long survival of the teachings, not just in the form of words but in the minds of those who have realized their meaning. He prays that the world be full of people with that kind of understanding maintaining faith in the Teacher, and in verse 56, that we uphold the key principle of dependent arising in the face of any adversity. Finally Tsongkhapa calls upon the worldly gods who delight in virtue, Brahma and Indra, upon the "worldly guardians," and then upon the protector deities of Buddhism—such as Mahakala, wrathful avatar of Avalokiteshvara—requesting that they also unwaveringly assist those authentically striving on the path.

Colophon

The Essence of Eloquence, Praise to the Supramundane Victor Buddha, Great Friend without Acquaintance to All the World, Foremost Teacher, for Teaching Profound Dependent Relativity was composed by Venerable Losang Dragpa, a monk who has heard many teachings, at Lhading, also called Nampar Gyalway Ling, at the hermitage of Lhashöl, "Beneath the Gods," of Oday Gungyal, mighty among the snowy peaks of the Land of Snows. The scribe was Namkha Pal.

Having defeated the four maras, having attained all excellent qualities, and having gone beyond both the world and solitary peace, Buddha is the "Supramundane Victor." Usually we only feel friendly toward people that we have some acquaintance with and who have some particular qualities that we favor. Buddha does not discriminate like that. Rather, he is a friend to everyone whoever they are, without prior scrutiny. Thus he is a "great friend without acquaintance" to the entire world. Lhashöl, the name of the hermitage, means "Beneath the Gods." Oday Gungyal is the name both of a great snow mountain and the local protector deity identified with it in Ölkha, in the region of Lhokha in southern Tibet.

When on that morning in 1398, in the solitude and silence of his retreat dwelling, under the protection of the deities of Oday Gungyal mountain, Tsongkhapa experienced the transcendent insight that is the stilling of fabrications and perfect peace, it was the outcome of years of extraordinary commitment. Tsongkhapa indeed stands out as a great scholar, an incisive intellect whose approach to the ultimate view was primarily through reasoned analysis. But he always combined study and teaching with intense practice. During the six years of retreat or semi-retreat that preceded his realization of the view, he offered hundreds of thousands of prostrations and prayer recitations in order to confess and purify negativities. He made a similarly huge number of mandala offerings to the buddhas in order to accumulate positive mental energy. He experienced many visions of deities and the great Indian masters of the lineage. In one vision Manjushri held his sword of wisdom with the hilt at his heart and the tip of the blade at Tsongkhapa's so that nectar flowed down the sword into Tsongkhapa's heart in a direct transmission of wisdom.

Tsongkhapa's lifetime achievement was therefore that of a true yogi. We need to utilize all our powers of mind if we want to follow his example. We need the power of trust in an exemplary teacher, the power of longing to be done with the world's superficial enticements, the power of ethical discipline, the power of universal love, the power of pliant, precisely focused concentration, the power of profound analysis, and the power of esoteric imagination on the tantric side.

A quality a little easier to cultivate than the above that we can all readily practice is the power of rejoicing. Rejoicing in the virtuous deeds of others is a simple way of accumulating positive energy for progress on the path. We may particularly rejoice in Tsongkhapa's genius, his eloquence, his devotion, and his dedication to the bodhisattva ideal, thanks to all of which the brilliance of Buddha's wisdom still shines forth in full radiance and the lion's roar of his utterance reverberates down to the present day.

9. Conclusion

L IFE IS A brief excursion; death is always the destination. We may grow strong, capable, resourceful, but still life balances on a tightrope. The disintegration that ends in death is inexorable. That which is gathered together in the aggregates is falling apart even now. The precious opportunity of our unpredictable and fleeting visit here must not be wasted. Yet under the dark spell of self-grasping, we sink into the gloom of confusion, our bright gleam of intelligence dims, and we remain distracted, blind to our unlimited evolutionary potential. The eloquent words of Tsongkhapa's song are a cascade of moonbeams to dispel that inner obscurity.

To derive real benefit from Buddha's teachings in fulfillment of the spirit in which they were given, we have to develop an interest in examining our mind. More than anything else, it is the mind that determines the way the world is; beyond all the more superficial causes of enjoyment and suffering, our mind is the ultimate factor that determines whether we are happy or not.

Buddha's marvelous presentation of dependent relativity and emptiness is contained in his doctrine of the two truths, conventional truth and ultimate truth. From this teaching we can derive an understanding of how the mind configures reality, observer and observed alike merely posited there in mutual dependence. If things lack even an iota of intrinsic establishment and are only designated by the interpreting mind, what does this imply about the nature of the mind? It begins to seem less a phenomenon thrown up by the abundant transformative powers of matter and more a force complementary to them, not inevitably bound by the physical limitations we presently experience.

Left dissatisfied by the thoroughly materialist outlook of the modern West, we come to see that we can most fruitfully guide our interactions with the world and its beings by relying on Buddha's doctrine of the four noble truths. There we find clearly described just how our involvement with the world and our fellow creatures becomes perverted into dissatisfaction, how we encounter happiness or suffering according to the extent to which our mind is caught in the tangles of the afflictions and karma, and how we can turn this situation around for ourselves and others. We may base our initial acceptance of the validity of the four truths on the veracity of the two truths. The latter teaching is undeniably reasonable, giving us a stable basis on which to establish trust in the Buddhist perspective and commit to a wholehearted venture on the path.

We use our Dharma knowledge to look within and combat the mara of the negative emotions. This inner approach is a practical, down-to-earth way to improve our prospects of happiness, as an alternative to investing all our hopes in the affairs of this world and in the limited comforts derived from acquiring things and manipulating our external circumstances. Negative emotions lead to contaminated actions, and such actions keep the wheel of cyclic existence turning. We should study the teachings on karma in order to be fully aware of the deep and long-term disadvantages of such actions. Whether we understand karma or not, we should recognize directly how uncomfortable such afflicted emotions make us and those around us feel here and now.

Through introspection and meditation, we become aware of why emotions like attachment, anger, pride, envy, and jealousy are negative. Simply by watching our mind in meditation alone, we will create a degree of detachment from the restless to and fro of our desires. This in itself is progress. Once we have identified the afflictive emotions as irrational states of mind that benefit no one, many of the explanations of dependent relativity and emptiness we have offered over the course of this book can be applied to reducing them. Even if at first we keep falling into an all-too-familiar ugly mood or unsuitable pattern of behavior, we are more alert to what is going on, and we determine to do better next time. Gradually, through thinking about and discussing such explanations, we understand how to apply the remedies indicated effectively.

We should always mix our own meditations with further study of Buddha's teachings in general and of the profound subject of dependent arising in particular. We can also assist our ability to connect with such subtle levels of meaning by accumulating a store of meritorious energy and by ridding ourselves of previously accumulated negative energy. Faith in our lama is another powerful positive force.

Accumulating merit and eliminating negativities are part of the practice of ethics, the first of the three higher trainings. Fundamentally, the practice of ethics, whether it is monastic discipline or avoiding the ten nonvirtues, is training yourself not to harm other sentient beings. Those who train in the bodhisattva ideal do not just avoid harming others; they try to help others in any way they can. Over time, such types of ethical training make the mind stable and firm and give much more chance of success to our efforts in the other two trainings, of concentration and wisdom. Training in concentration involves developing the mind to the point where it can stay focused single-mindedly on any chosen object without wavering or becoming tired. With a mind like that our wisdom investigations will be sharp and penetrating. It is important to practice both of the latter trainings, concentration and wisdom. Traditionally it is said that if we have less time, we should focus on the training of concentration, whereas if we have more time to study in depth, then we should put more emphasis on the training in wisdom at the beginning.

Those of us who have more time to spend on the training of wisdom take more teachings and study more texts, but still we must mix these activities with our own analysis and meditation. We should take care that the texts we use are authentic ones written by those who are skilled in the subject, because anything good always has its shoddy imitations. We should not dismiss the views of the lower schools but rather practice trying to see things from their perspectives. Sharpening our mind on the lower schools' systems is an excellent preparation for cutting through to the unparalleled insights of the Consequentialist view. In meditation we can start with the view of the lower schools and work up to the view of the highest school. It is also useful to perform this type of meditation in reverse order, starting off with the most subtle object of refutation and working down the scale to the grossest.

We should always keep to the fore the aim of realizing emptiness proper though. Realizing emptiness must put one beyond disappointment, humiliation, and frustration. Everything is empty and thus equal in that way. Deep meditative absorption into the subtlest form of emptiness is the one experience that will actually dissolve away forever the mind's most ingrained disruptive tendencies. In *Praise for Dependent Relativity*, as each joyful, succinct praise of Buddha succeeds the last, Tsongkhapa impresses on us again and again that only the moon rays of the wisdom of the emptiness that is thoroughly compatible and harmonious with dependent relativity have that ultimate healing power. This alone is the version of emptiness for which the logical case is flawless.

Whatever Dharma practice we engage in, from contemplative retreat to directly helping others, we should never expect some marvelous effect to occur in just a short time. "Abandon hope for results" is excellent advice. Grasping at achieving Dharma realizations is a sure way to hinder their occurring and can lead to all sorts of false pride and despondency. We should strive to do our best and attain the ideals Buddha set forth without having fixed expectations about when that might happen. We strive for these objectives simply because they are the most worth striving for. Life will always be too short, but we will die having been single-minded in the greatest venture.

What we need is a stable and firm type of practice. What we have in our mind now are stable and firm tendencies toward various delusions. When we practice Dharma we build up predispositions toward virtue and wisdom. By practicing well over long periods of time, these predispositions become stable and strong in our mind. If someone carved a Buddha image out of a boulder, then we would expect it to last for a long time. On the other hand, if someone simply painted a Buddha image on the rock, less effort would be involved, but rain and other elements would soon destroy it. In our Dharma practice we should aim to be like the person who sculpts the stone, making the extra effort for the sake of an enduring result.

Even though the weeds of delusion sprout profusely in our mind at the moment, these delusions are based on a misunderstanding of reality, so they are not impossible to uproot. As soon as we achieve a clear understanding, our ignorance must give way, like night before day. The predispositions we develop when we meditate on dependent arising are very stable because they are based on reality. And because they are based on truth, there is every reason to hope they will ripen up into realization. Then, by prolonged acquaintance with and meditation on this, the ultimate of truths, we can escape from the clutches of all four maras once and for all.

Thus confident that the results of practicing these teachings of the Enlightened One passed down through Nagarjuna, Chandrakirti, and Tsongkhapa will be very beneficial, we should enter into the practice of them with a relaxed and happy attitude. When we become more deeply acquainted with them, we may reach the conclusion that there is nothing more beneficial for wandering beings than them, in which case we will approach them with gladness and rejoicing. Then our practice of Dharma will be a pleasure. There are various reasons why we might study these teachings with great seriousness: because they are very profound and need plenty of careful thought; because they are the gateway to the highest wisdom; or because they precipitate in us a fundamental change of heart, away from the addictions of cyclic existence. Nonetheless, a tight, tense mind will only be a hindrance, so we should keep our mind happy and relaxed throughout: at the beginning, in the middle, and at the end. Then, with steady persistence, all the fruits of the path will be ours.

Notes

1. Joseph Huc, *Travels in Tartary, Thibet and China*, translated by W. Hazlitt, 2 vols. (London: 1851; reprint Delhi: Asian Educational Services, 1998), vol. 1, p. 225.
2. Ibid., vol. 2, pp. 46–48.
3. The first line of verse 1 in Tibetan reads *gang zhig gzigs shing gsung ba yis.* I have gone along with Ngawang Puntsog and others' insistence on this reading in preference to the often-found *gang zhig gzigs shing gsung ba yi*—"Of what you realized and proclaimed." The former makes better sense. See Gen Lam-rimpa Ngawang Puntsog, *Eliminating the Darkness of Extremism: A Commentary to "Praise for Dependent Relativity"* (*Rten 'brel bstod pa'i 'grel pa mthar 'dzin mun sel*), in *Blo bzang dgongs rgyan mu tig phreng mdzes deb,* vol. 4 (Mundgod: Drepung Loseling Educational Society, 1995), p. 104.
4. This paragraph was inspired by a remark by Karl Popper in Karl R. Popper and John C. Eccles, *The Self and Its Brain* (Berlin: Springer-Verlag, 1977), p. 120.
5. Information from Michael Klesius, "Search for a Cure: Amid the Unrelenting Spread of AIDS," *National Geographic*, Feb. 2002.

About the Authors

Lobsang Gyatso

Born in Tibet in 1928, Lobsang Gyatso studied at Drepung Loseling Monastery near Lhasa. As a refugee in India, he became a leading figure in the education of Tibetan youth in exile and in the transmission of Tibetan Buddhist philosophy to the West. He was principal of the Institute of Buddhist Dialectics from its establishment in 1973 until his death in 1997.

Graham Woodhouse

Born in England in 1952, Graham Woodhouse received full ordination as a Buddhist monk in the Tibetan tradition from His Holiness the Dalai Lama in 1994. He studied for seventeen years at the Institute of Buddhist Dialectics in Dharamsala and received his geshe degree from Drepung Loseling Monastery in 2006.

About Wisdom Publications

WISDOM PUBLICATIONS is dedicated to offering works relating to and inspired by Buddhist traditions.

To learn more about us or to explore our other books, please visit our website at www.wisdompubs.org.

You can subscribe to our e-newsletter or request our print catalog online, or by writing to:

Wisdom Publications
199 Elm Street
Somerville, Massachusetts 02144 USA

You can also contact us at 617-776-7416, or info@wisdompubs.org.

Wisdom is a nonprofit, charitable 501(c)(3) organization and donations in support of our mission are tax deductible.

Wisdom Publications is affiliated with the Foundation for the Preservation of the Mahayana Tradition (FPMT).